SOCCER RULES
EXPLAINED

Photo: Phil Stephens.

SOCCER RULES EXPLAINED

Stanley Lover

Foreword by
J. S. Blatter
General Secretary, FIFA

THE LYONS PRESS

Also by *Stanley Lover;*
Soccer Laws Illustrated
Soccer Match Control
Soccer Judge
Soccer and Its Rules
You are the Ref!
Illustrated Soccer Quiz Book

Published simultaneously in the United Kingdom by Eric Dobby Publishing Ltd,

10   9   8   7   6   5   4   3   2   1

Library of Congress Cataloging-in-Publication Data

Lover, Stanley F.
Soccer rules explained : the game and new rules / Stanley Lover ;
Foreword by J.S. Blatter
p. cm.
"With the laws of the game and decisions of the International Football Association Board, reproduction authorised by Fédération internationale de football association."
ISBN 1-55821-722-3
1. Soccer - - Rules.   I. Fédération internationale de football association.
II. Title.
GV943.4.L686   1998
796.334'02'022--dc21
97-51734   CIP

Printed in Hong Kong
Typeset in 10pt on 13pt Garamond by Kevin O'Connor
Illustrations by Stanley Lover

Contents

Foreword

Sepp Blatter. Photo: FIFA

The title alone of this book guarantees its success. The followers of our sport are constantly increasing in number and are eager to enjoy it to the fullest.

Explaining the Laws in such a clear and simple way is not easy. This publication manages to do so and its future readers, which we hope will be numerous, will undoubtedly benefit in more ways than one from the new information gleaned from it.

J.S. Blatter
FIFA General Secretary

See the Cat!

A Preface

You have probably seen those paintings of beautiful landscapes where the artist has mischievously hidden the form or image of an animal - often the face of a cat. Not immediately visible to the naked eye, the image suddenly becomes clear when the eye tunes into the mind of the artist. Then it's easy to see.

However, no matter how hard some observers try they cannot tune in without help. This was the case of Mr Rapier who wrote to Clay Berling, the proprietor of *Soccer America*. Mr Rapier had practised several sports but became a newcomer to the soccer world when taking on a talented, soccer-playing stepson. After watching many soccer games, in person or via videos, he confessed to Clay Berling that he could not "see" the fascination of soccer. A willing pupil, Mr Rapier appealed for help.

To master player, Pelé and other soccer folk, soccer is "The Beautiful Game". As is said, beauty is in the eye of the beholder. Soccer people seem to have no problem identifying the beauty in the game - the cat in the painting so to speak. How can we help Mr Rapier and others unlock the door to soccer passion? Where is that cat in the soccer landscape?

The answer is - it's everywhere! Sometimes visible as a kitten purring over subtle skills, athletic grace, intelligent moves; reacting to tidal waves of emotion with buckets of tears of joy or misfortune; or, as a lion, exploding with a thunderous roar at a dramatic moment.

"Our cat" is never still. Involved in all the action, he's a kicking, running, jumping, heading, scrapping cat with flying fur and scratching claws. We see him in the interaction between player and ball, the combining of minds and bodies in the ebb and flow of team play. He's there at every challenge for possession, every disagreement between judge and judged.

To help Mr Rapier and friends see the game through the eyes of the soccer cat we look at the way the game is intended to be played according to the landscape painted by its founders. The "hidden cat" is draped in brushstrokes of philosophy, discipline, character, respect and all of those qualities of fair play which signpost world citizens through life.

Our reference is the code of play, the rules of the game, for without a written creed there is confusion and chaos. The soccer creed has stood the test of time since its birth in 1863. It has provided a fun game binding millions into one world soccer family.

In artistic language we will take the formal, somewhat cold and legalistic text as our canvas, applying colour with explanatory brushstrokes, to reproduce that "Beautiful Game" landscape with the face of the cat easily recognised.

Thank you, Mr Rapier, for your appeal, and thanks to Clay Berling for emphasising the need for *Soccer Explained*.

Stanley Lover
August 1997

Introduction

Something strange was happening at the giant Workers' Stadium. Peking were playing Tientsin before 40,000 fans who applauded enthusiastically but the applause seemed to be related to a match being played somewhere else in China because it often occurred when there was no action on the field. Play had been stopped for a free kick when an announcement was broadcast provoking appreciative reaction from the fans.

An interpreter explained the mystery by pointing to a person seated at a table close to the touch line. "He is the person giving the commentary. He is one of our leading referees and is explaining the decisions of the match referee, Dr Wong, who is a professor of physical culture."

As the game proceeded the interpreter gave a summary of the commentary:

"No. 6 obstructed an opponent. Dr Wong has awarded an indirect free kick and is confirming the decision with one arm raised above his head."

"The goal was not allowed because Dr Wong noticed that No. 10 handled the ball. He has awarded a direct free kick to Tientsin."

"Dr Wong has signalled permission for the Peking medical assistant to enter the field to examine the injury to No. 6. He has stopped his watch so that no playing time is lost."

"Offside. No. 7 was in an offside position at the moment the ball was passed towards him. The referee considered that he was interfering with play and has awarded an indirect free kick to Peking. Notice, again, the signal - one arm raised above the head."

"Although that was not an intentional foul Dr Wong considered that it was too dangerous to the opponent. Indirect free kick."

There was no doubt that the fans welcomed this additional insight into the game as seen through the eyes of an expert. They understood why the match was stopped and the appropriate action required by the laws. Their appreciation was such that the match officials were applauded more than the players!

It is not practical to consider a similar commentary for **all** soccer games but the experience made the point that fans, and players, want to know more about what is happening in their match.

Many players will confess that they play through their soccer lives without giving much thought to the laws because the game is simple and it is the job of the referee to apply the laws. If it were a fact that players and spectators accepted referees' decisions without dissent this attitude would be reasonable but, in practice, much confusion and irritation are generated when perfectly sound decisions are misinterpreted due to lack of knowledge of the laws to which the game must be played. Players also miss the opportunity of achieving full potential by not appreciating how to use the laws to their advantage. For example, a forward with exciting talent for scoring goals loses a chance to demonstrate his skills every time he is penalised for offside. On some occasions it is difficult to avoid being offside but, with a clear understanding of why the law is there and how offside can be avoided the player can improve his own performance and contribute more to the success of his team.

It is clearly sensible to advise all involved in soccer to read the Laws of the Game but to open the law book is to enter forbidding territory because of the dry-as-dust legal terminology which is necessary to bear credible translation into other languages. The official laws can bore all but the most dedicated student.

The purpose of the book is to open a new window on the Game of Soccer by providing an easy-to-read guide to the game itself, to how the laws were formulated, to discover the reason and wisdom behind formal phrases and the practical interpretations seen in every match.

After a brief review of the pleasures of playing and watching soccer, and a background to its laws, there follows an explanation of each law by way of an introduction to the official text.

Whatever your role and experience in the game the contents of this book are intended to add a new perspective to future matches in the form of your own commentary on the events of play as revealed to the 40,000 fans and players in the Workers' Stadium, Peking, China.

The magic of a ball. A friend for life. Photo: Henri Swarc

Acknowledgements

The author and publishers acknowledge, with pleasure, the support of FIFA in granting permission to reproduce the official Laws of the Game, approved signals and other material.

1
The Game of Soccer

Why soccer attracts millions

There has to be something really special about a game with 40 million players spread throughout 200 countries. A game which counts among its followers young and old, male and female, all creeds, classes, colours, nationalities and political persuasions. A game which touches the life of practically every person on this earth, in one way or another, when one tournament, the FIFA World Cup, comes to its climax.

What is so special about soccer? What makes it the world's most popular sport?

First things first. Why "soccer"? What does the name mean? Officially the game is "Association Football", being the description adopted in 1863 when a handful of clubs met in London to agree on a common set of rules of play. From this The Football Association was founded.

"Soccer" is a word attributed to Charles Wreford-Brown, one of the game's early amateur gentlemen players. Known by friends as "Reefer" he was an outstanding sportsman. An England soccer international in the late 1890s, "Reefer" Brown also played top-class rugby and cricket. When seasons overlapped he would play whichever sport pleased him. One day a friend asked, "Are you playing rugger today?" (Rugger was, and still is, another word for rugby football.) In reply "Reefer" Brown said, "No, I'm playing soccer", a playword of "association". He could have said "footer", another popular description, but "soccer" has become established particularly in countries where other forms of football are played such as Rugby Union, Rugby League, American and Australian Rules Football.

The game of soccer was born out of an ancient communal ceremony where hundreds of participants engaged in a rough and tumble scramble for a ball with the object of moving it to a defined target. Other forms of ball games, practised in China, Greece, Italy, France, etc. have influenced the formation of the modern game of soccer.

Today's game is a joy to play because each player can demonstrate personal skills. It is a joy to watch because the ball is always visible and easy to follow.

While a formal game requires two teams of eleven players, much fun can be had from kick-a-about games with fewer players.

Playing is appealing enough but soccer attracts non-players who enjoy the spectacle of colour, athleticism, constant ebb and flow of play, the heroes and the villains. Watchers become involved whether the game is at schoolboy level, in the park, or is part of the carnival atmosphere of a World Cup event. Deep passions are aroused as watchers share emotional ties with supporters of club or national teams.

Undoubtedly the players are the main attraction. With a ball they can thrill us with clever skills, breathtaking spontaneity, enviable agility. Exceptionally gifted players become soccer gods, their names inscribed in soccer history, each worshipped by successive generations of soccer folk.

A vital element to soccer's attraction, possibly *the* vital element, is the object used in the game - the ball. For what would a soccer god be without a ball? Just an ordinary human being!

Why should the ball be so significant? The laws require that, "the ball shall be spherical". A wise choice because a sphere is a psychological symbol having pleasant associations with the Earth, Sun and Moon. Spherical objects, chosen specially to represent the powers of the Sun, have been used for centuries in rituals to ensure good harvests.

Soccer is a form of tribal ceremony very evident at important matches involving thousands of supporters. Tribal customs include collective chants, wearing good luck symbols, mass gestures and, in some countries, the performing of witchcraft to keep away evil spirits.

Almost from birth we develop an hypnotic attraction for a ball, one of our first toys. Present any child with a ball and the reaction is immediate - a smile. An inanimate object and yet it comes alive with a slight touch. It will rarely be still, being pushed, rolled, bounced, thrown or kicked into dynamic action. A ball is smooth, comfortable to hold and becomes a friend for life.

Games with a ball have been around since the beginning of time. Playing with one combines the fascination of a sphere with an expression of physical ability. The ball reproduces and measures personal skill.

The game of soccer is special because it unites these charms into a disciplined sporting contest.

Football in the Middle Ages. Entertainment of the common people, a noisy tough tussle in the streets.

How soccer is played

Before discussing the laws which regulate play it may be helpful to outline the object of the game and how it is played.

A game of soccer is a match between two teams, each having eleven players, with the object of moving a ball between two targets (goals). The players may use any part of the body, except the hands, to control or propel the ball.

One player of each team is designated as a keeper of the goal (goalkeeper) and may use the hands to prevent the ball from passing through the goal. Goalkeepers wear colours different from the other players so that it is clear who may handle the ball.

The team which makes the highest number of goals wins the match. If there are no goals, or an equal goal count, the match is a draw .

Game rules specify the size and markings of the field of play,

The passing game.

The powerful kick.

A fair challenge for possession of the ball.

A fair tackle playing the ball.

Control.

The dribble.

The heading duel.

The spectacular volley.

Heading for goal.

components required, time limits, procedures - and disciplines to be followed.

There is no fixed formation of players. The goalkeeper, because of his role, stays near to the goal but outfield players have freedom of movement. According to preference, ability or tactics, players adopt certain positions in defence, mid-field or attack. They may interchange positions freely although in most levels of soccer some degree of specialization develops.

On the field each team is limited to eleven players but an additional seven players may be nominated as possible substitutes. Not more than three may be used under the rules of a competition but for other games a maximum of five may be allowed.

When the ball is in play every player has the right to challenge for possession. This may involve varying degrees of physical contact between opponents. This is allowed providing it is fair and not dangerous.

Individual skills in playing with the ball, such as control, running, kicking, heading, passing it to a team mate, contribute to the overall team effort in moving the ball towards and through the opponent's goal.

A neutral person, a referee, is on the field to apply the procedures and disciplines required by the rules of play. He may be supported by two officials, each carrying a flag and patrolling a touch line, to assist with decisions relating to the ball crossing the boundary lines or offside.

The referee controls play with a whistle and arm signals.

The pleasure of playing soccer

The foregoing outline indicates the simplicity of the game. It is also an emotional experience. For the player, anticipation and excitement of an enjoyable activity starts when a soccer game is announced, be it hours, days or weeks in advance. The journey to the field, meeting team mates, engaging in soccer talk in a friendly atmosphere make for a special occasion.

Changing from everyday clothes into colourful soccer strip is like taking on a new personality, satisfying a natural desire to dress up to play a role. In the dressing-room a unique mixture of sights, sounds and smells sets nerves tingling similar to the pre-curtain tension experienced by stage artists.

Although a close comradeship exists some players may show signs of acute nervous anxiety. One of the world's greatest players, Sir Stanley Matthews, who played professional soccer from 16 to 50 years of age, admitted to being physically sick before some of his matches.

Running onto a soccer field, particularly in front of many fans, is another special moment although it may add to anxiety. However, all prematch nerves are calmed at the first touch of the ball. Concentration can now be focussed on the game ahead.

During the match soccer pleasure mounts with increasing mental and physical exertions needed to solve problems arising from constantly changing action. All attention and movement is centred on the ball. It seems to radiate invisible signals to the players like expanding ripples caused by a stone dropping into a calm lake. Each player interprets the signals according to individual ability while being conscious of his role as a member of a team. Instant decisions are necessary after assessing the best position to meet the next phase of play, whether to move close to an opponent to reduce his effectiveness or to go for the ball, to cover a team mate, how best to control the ball coming fast at an awkward angle with only a split second before contact. When in possession a quick evaluation of options available is needed before deciding to run with the ball, move it to a team mate, try to pass an opponent or take a shot at goal.

Emotions fluctuate with successes and failures, from great elation

Sir Stanley Matthews, 'The Prince of Dribblers'. A world professional star from 16 to 50 years of age.

when your team scores to despair when a goal is lost. The end of the match brings congratulations, commiserations, and an inquest into the main events of play, all in an atmosphere charged with another unique mixture of sights, sounds and smells.

Whatever the result leaving for home gives time for reflection leading to a degree of satisfaction in having taken part in a sporting contest, sharing an emotional experience with friends and counting the days to the next match.

The pleasure of watching soccer

Soccer games have always attracted spectators whether in the form of one man and his dog strolling in the park or the estimated 200,000 fanatics who stormed the Wembley Stadium gates to see the 1923 FA Cup Final between West Ham United and Bolton Wanderers.

In the first century of its existence soccer has been well supported by millions attending matches, mostly under primitive conditions. The supporter has often been treated as a necessary evil even when paying for the privilege of standing on cramped terraces exposed to the worst of winter elements. References to spectators in soccer laws were concerned with "interference with the play, misconduct and misdemeanours".

One, seemingly grudging, recognition that spectators may wish to enjoy the game appeared for many years at the end of a note in which referees were advised not to constantly stop play "for trifling or doubtful offences" as this can cause bad feeling among players and "spoils the pleasure of spectators".

Soccer is now being presented as an entertainment package with Olympic-style ceremonies and show-biz sparkle to keep fans happy enough to behave themselves. A remarkable expansion of televised soccer has attracted vast audiences to the point where more people watch soccer from the comfort of their homes than from the sidelines.

The degree of pleasure to be gained from watching the game itself varies according to knowledge and experience. Newcomers may be content to be carried along with the general atmosphere created by a group of enthusiastic sportsmen chasing a ball. For the very sound reasons already given, relating to the magnetic attraction of a ball, newcomers will find it difficult to take their eyes off the ball and think that the object of the game is to kick it aimlessly up and down the field until someone puts it into a goal. Well, that's not a bad start. With more exposure to the game comes knowledge and more pleasure.

Players, and ex-players, get their pleasure from watching based on an inner knowledge of "can do, have done". They identify with the physical effort, the skills and techniques. Every touch of the ball has a personal meaning whether it be instant control, an accurate pass, a shot at goal or, even, a miskick! Many can appreciate the cut and thrust of tactical play, decision making ability, ball control skills, timing of challenges.

The connoisseur quickly identifies the real stars, potential troublemakers, the weak referee. He calculates the outcome of each phase of play, revising forecasts as the tactical scene changes.

The connoisseur acts out the roles of the player, the coach, referee and the fan. He can be seen participating with reactive body language to resist a crunching tackle, swaying to deceive an opponent or thrusting his head forward to nod the ball into goal.

For him the game is much more than moving a ball between two goals, it is total immersion in the charms of what he calls "The Beautiful Game".

Soccer for women

"The Beautiful Game" counts among its admirers millions of women with over one million registered players.

Women have played soccer since the 14th century but regular teams began to appear only 500 years later. In today's world women's soccer is highly organised with established leagues and international tournaments. Administrators of women's soccer have battled incessantly for official recognition and their efforts were finally rewarded when FIFA decided, in 1991, to form a special committee responsible for women's soccer on a global basis.

A new page in soccer history was turned when, in the same year, FIFA organised the first FIFA World Championship for Women's Football, in China. The tournament attracted huge interest after it was seen to be played to a surprising level of skill with only slight differences in the laws concerning the size of the ball and duration of play.

Women in soccer, the fashion in the first match played by the British Ladies Football Club was nightcaps, skirts, shinguards and heavy boots (1895).

The World number one woman player, Michelle Akers-Stahl, star of the USA team which won the historic First Women's World Championship, China, 1991. Photo: Phil Stephens.

An astute move by FIFA because today's women soccer players will be the mothers of tomorrow's soccer children, educated to appreciate the special qualities of the game.

2
Background to Soccer Law

The role of soccer law

The original role of soccer law was to provide a uniform code of rules for several similar ball games played in universities, clubs and colleges during the 19th century. A simple role but many years were to pass before a universal code was agreed. Successive generations of legislators have refined its text without changing basic principles or ethics.

Today the role of soccer law is just about perfect. It provides a simple game which can be played within the physical limits of any person. It can be played anywhere with inexpensive equipment, with time and space for players to develop individual skills inside a team sport, in a healthy environment and be attractive enough to arouse the passions of millions of spectators.

The game of soccer is very special because its laws have very special qualities.

Need for a common code

Modern soccer can be played by millions but when the founders of the game met to decide on a common code of play they were concerned only to satisfy the needs of a few English public schools and universities. During the early 1800s these important institutions combined sports with moral instruction to prepare future leaders of the nation's business, government and military services, for the responsibilities ahead.

Football was one of the sports chosen to harden bodies, test courage, develop self-discipline and promote sound ethics. Each school had its own form of game according to the facilities available. The London schools of Charterhouse and Westminster, restricted to play in small cloisters, favoured a dribbling game. Cheltenham and Rugby used the space of open fields to play a more scrambling game similar to early mob-street football.

The need for a common method of play arose when students passed on to university. Attempts to organise football games ended in chaos because the undergraduates played to the rules of their own public school. Thus it was that a committee was set up at Cambridge University to devise a game which would incorporate the best features of the variations practised by the public schools.

The main issue was to decide between moving the ball by kicking and dribbling or running with it and allowing physical assaults on opponents to gain possession. The vote went in favour of the former probably because of the argument that mature players, in professions with heavy responsibilities, would be discouraged from playing for fear of serious injury.

Although the first common rules, known as the Cambridge Rules, were intended to resolve an internal problem they were to become a major source of reference when a universal code was adopted in 1863 by the newly formed Football Association.

Football had now turned away from the roughness, violence and confusion of the mob-style methods to a more open game giving the players opportunities to display skills with the ball and to encourage tactical development in team play.

Organisation and skill are the main differences between ancient and modern forms of soccer. We shall see how current laws spell out the simple basics required to organise a game and how players are able to demonstrate their skills.

Who controls the laws?

Tradition is important in soccer. The game has grown to global popularity due not only to the wisdom of the founders of an attractive sport but also to the spreading of its virtues to many countries by British soldiers, sailors, teachers, industrialists, etc.

The British contribution is recognised in the composition of the body which controls soccer law, the International Football Association

The great influence of public school football. Captured here in a match between Charterhouse and Old Cartusian Internationals in 1892. Note the referee in white and an umpire in formal dress and school cap. The sixth player from the left is "Reefer" Brown, who is thought to have invented the word "soccer".

RULES

Passed at International Conference held in London, June, 1886.

1.—That this Board shall be called "THE INTERNATIONAL FOOTBALL ASSOCIATION BOARD," and shall be composed of two representatives from each of the four national associations.

2.—That the Board shall meet each year in the month of June at the invitation of each of the national associations in the order of seniority.

3.—That at such meeting one of the representatives of the association convening the same shall preside, and the other shall act as secretary.

4.—That the minute-book of the meetings shall be fully entered up by the secretary, and shall be forwarded to the association next in turn before the 1st of January ensuing.

5.—That business shall not be proceeded with unless a majority of the associations be represented.

6.—That resolutions shall not be adopted unless agreed to by three-fourths of those present; but in the case of alterations of laws of the game, a unanimous vote shall be necessary.

7.—That the Board shall discuss and decide proposed alterations in the laws of the game and generally any matters affecting Association football in its international relations

8.—That the committees of the various national associations shall forward in writing, on or before 1st February each year, to the secretary of the association entitled to convene the next meeting, any suggestions or alterations deemed desirable, which shall be printed and distributed on or before 1st March, for consideration at the annual general meetings of the association.

9.—That decisions of this Board shall be at once binding on all the associations, and no alterations in the laws of the game made by any association shall be valid until accepted by this Board.

The next International Conference will be held at Glasgow in June, 1887.

First Rules of the International Football Board. Photo: FIFA.

Board. The four British associations of England, Scotland, Ireland, and Wales, are partners with FIFA (Fédération Internationale de Football Association) in forming the Board. FIFA is a federation of over 200 national football associations. Its objects are to promote and control the game, to foster friendly relations, to prevent discrimination and to decide differences which may arise between national associations.

The International Board meets annually to discuss and decide proposed alterations to the Laws of the Game and any other matters referred to it by its members. Since its formation in 1886 by the four British associations joined in 1913 by FIFA, the International Board has been extremely conservative when considering the many suggestions received each year. Its policy is to make changes only when there is positive evidence that change is necessary.

In recent years the IB has amended certain laws to combat undesirable trends in the game which have put undue emphasis on defensive tactics and excess physical contact. The role of the goalkeeper has caused concern resulting in restrictions intended to make the ball more available to outfield players. Time-wasting, violent tackles, deliberate foul play and handling of the ball, now incur severe punishments. Various experiments have been authorised to test ideas for changes but results have to be very conclusive before the IB will agree to any modification.

Changes can only occur when agreed by at least three-quarters of the total of eight votes held in the proportion of one each for the four British Associations and four votes for FIFA. Effectively there can be no change without the support of FIFA.

Deliberations of the IB are notified to all national associations in the form of an amendment to law, a decision which clarifies a certain aspect of a law, instructions, or advice, together with reasons and hoped-for effect. Much care is taken to compile announcements in formal English capable of accurate translation into all world languages. Sometimes it is difficult to avoid a legalistic style which makes for heavy reading - a major reason for the need of this book!

Interpretations and clarifications of the laws are published in the form of questions and answers. These deal with official queries submitted by national associations and represent soccer case law.

FIFA Organisation

Congress
Executive Committee
General Secretariat
Confederations

- AFRICA
- ASIA
- South AMERICA
- N & Central AMERICA
- OCEANIA
- EUROPE

Organisation of FIFA.

A selection of questions and official answers is included at the end of this book.

As guardians of the law members of the International Board are required to exercise practical wisdom in weighing up the probable consequences of proposed changes. They are concerned not only with technicalities of play but also with preserving the moral character-forming qualities intended by the founders of the game.

3
Soccer Laws Explained

Definition

"Law; a rule prescribed by authority", is a very dull definition in any context. There seems little connection between this word and the exciting, vibrant, colourful spectacle of a game of soccer and yet, without law, or rules, there can be no game, no organisation, no guiding principles, no discipline, no control, no interest and no fun.

The fact that soccer has intoxicated the world proves that the formula to which it is played, i.e. the laws of the game, must have some special qualities. We shall see how simple these qualities are and how they appear in every kick, and every facet of play.

Construction of soccer law

We have seen how modern soccer emerged out of ancient forms of ball games because the confusion of different interpretations spelt out the need for a common formula. The original laws, adopted in 1863, comprised just fourteen short paragraphs and eight definitions. The basic text of modern soccer law was devised by Sir Stanley Rous in 1938. For nearly 60 years the fundamentals remained intact but amendments and additions, mostly in the form of explanations and instructions to cover practical situations, made the law book into a forbidding document.

A new approach was overdue when, in 1997, the IFAB adopted a much reduced text. It dispensed with some of the superfluous and repetitive wordage and put basic law into a more presentable format.

However, the revised text still includes unnecessary repetition and leaves much to be read between the lines. For longtime students of soccer this is no big problem but, for future generations of soccer

I.

The maximum **length of the ground** shall be 200 yards, the maximum **breadth** shall be 100 yards, the length and breadth shall be marked off with flags and the **goal** shall be defined by two upright posts, 8 yards apart, without any tap or bar across them.

II.

The Game shall be commenced by a **place kick** from the centre of the ground by the side winning the toss, the other side shall not approach within 10 yards of the ball until it is kicked off. After a goal is won the losing side shall be entitled to kick off.

III.

The two sides shall change goals after each goal is won.

IV.

A goal shall be won when the ball passes over the space between the goal posts (at whatever height), not being thrown, knocked on, or carried.

V.

When the ball is in **touch** the first player who touches it shall kick or throw it from the point on the boundary line where it left the ground, in a direction at right angles with the boundary line.

VI.

A player shall be **out of play** immediately he is in front of the ball, and must return behind the ball as soon as possible. If the ball is kicked past a player by his own side, he shall not touch or kick it or advance until one of the other side has first kicked it or one of his own side on a level with or in front of him has been able to kick it.

VII.

In case the ball goes behind the goal line, if a player on the side to whom the goal belongs first touches the ball, one of his side shall be entitled to a free kick from the goal line at the point opposite the place where the ball shall be touched. If a player of the opposite side first touches the ball, one of his side shall be entitled to a free kick from a point 15 yards outside the goal line, opposite the place where the ball is touched.

The Laws of the Game as they were finally adopted by The Football Association in December 1863. Photo: FIFA.

VIII.

If a player makes a **fair catch** he shall be entitled to a **free kick**, provided l claims it by making a mark with his heel at once; and in order to take such kick he ma go as far back as he pleases, and no player on the opposite side shall advance beyond h mark until he has kicked.

IX.

A player shall be entitled to run with the ball towards his adversaries' goal if l makes a fair catch, or catches the ball on the first bound; but in the case of a fair catch, he makes his mark, he shall not then run.

X.

If any player shall run with the ball towards his adversaries' goal, any player on th opposite side shall be at liberty to charge, hold, trip, or hack him, or to wrest the ball fro him; but no player shall be held and hacked at the same time.

XI.

Neither tripping or hacking shall be allowed, and no player shall use his hand r elbows to hold or push his adversary, except in the case provided for by Law X.

XII.

Any player shall be allowed to charge another, provided they are both in active play. A player shall be allowed to charge if even he is out of play.

XIII.

A player shall be allowed to throw the ball or pass it to another if he make a fair catch, or catches the ball on the first bound.

XIV.

No player shall be allowed to wear projecting nails, iron plates, or gutta percha he soles or heels of his boots.

DEFINITION OF TERMS.

A Place Kick—Is a Kick at the Ball while it is on the ground, in any position which the Kicker may choose to place it.

A Free Kick—Is the privilege of Kicking the Ball, without obstruction, in such manner as the Kicker may think fit.

A Fair Catch—Is when the Ball is Caught, after it has touched the person of an Adversary or has been kicked, knocked on, or thrown by an Adversary, and before it has touched the ground or one of the Side catching it; but if the Ball is kicked from out of touch, or from behind goal line, a fair Catch cannot be made.

Hacking—Is kicking an Adversary on the front of the leg, below the knee.

Tripping—Is throwing an Adversary by the use of the legs without the hands, and without hacking or charging.

Charging—Is attacking an Adversary with the shoulder, chest, or body, without using the hands or legs.

Knocking on—Is when a Player strikes or propels the Ball with his hands, arms or body, without kicking or throwing it.

Holding—Includes the obstruction of a Player by the hand or any part of the arm below the elbow.

Touch—Is that part of the field, on either side of the ground, which is beyond the line of flags.

players, coaches, match officials and other participants, separate edicts are needed to answer questions of practical interpretation.

Until these are available, digested and understood, read on!

Basic principles

Despite the formidable nature of the mass of law and appendices the whole becomes easy to understand when the principles on which it is based are clear, i.e. the spirit behind the written word. These are simply equality, safety and enjoyment.

Equality

Every player is entitled to an equal opportunity to demonstrate personal skills. The laws provide protection for players of all abilities by restricting the degree of physical contact when contesting possession of the ball.

Safety

To enable players to engage in a healthy sport, all elements of danger are strictly controlled.

Enjoyment

To promote maximum enjoyment of the game, all who take part are required to observe an honourable code of discipline and fair play.

Law groups

Before getting to the detail of each law there are logical relationships and groupings as follows:

Components: Field - Ball - Players - Players' Equipment (Laws 1, 2, 3, 4)

Control: Referees - Assistant Referees (Laws 5, 6)

Game rules: Duration - Start and Restart of Play - Ball In and Out of Play - Scoring (Laws 7, 8, 9, 10)

Technical: Offside (Law 11)

Discipline: Fouls and Misconduct (Law 12)

Restarts: Free kicks - Penalty kick - Throw-in - Goal kick - Corner kick (Laws 13, 14, 15, 16, 17)

In the next section the official Laws of the Game are published with an introduction to each of the groups noted above. Before the formal text of the law and International Board Decisions appears a commentary on the most important points of each law.

How to study the laws

The degree of knowledge you wish to acquire from a study of the laws depends on your interest or role in the game. A referee needs to study every word and know its interpretation whereas a player, coach, administrator, journalist or fan, can ignore much detail such as dimensions and technical specifications.

Whatever your interest you can obtain the most value from the time devoted to study if you establish priorities:

1 First priority - what you must know: basic facts of each law - its function (see groups) - why the game is stopped - punishment - how the game is restarted, etc.

2. Second priority - what you should know: relevant decisions - examples of special situations.
3. Third priority - matters of interest: cases from questions and answers.

The laws are formal and flexible. Formalities are clearly stated ". . . the field of play must be rectangular", "names of substitutes must be given to the referee . ." etc. Flexibility is allowed for friendly matches (e.g. number of substitutes, youth, veteran and women's soccer, size of ball, duration of game, etc.).

National associations are permitted a certain discretion, e.g. minimum number of players in a team, and some special rules apply for international matches, e.g. size of field.

There is much reason and wisdom within the laws. The basic principles of equality, safety and enjoyment become evident if each statement is questioned with the key word "WHY?". Why must the field be of oblong shape? Why must the ball be spherical? Why must opponents remain at least ten yards from the ball at free kicks? Why offside?

To analyse the content of each law in this manner puts a fresh meaning on that dull word "law" because we can appreciate the intentions of the founders, followed by successive generations of legislators, to make the game simple and enjoyable with the emphasis on preserving the moral character-forming qualities of a healthy sport played with passion while respecting the spirit of fair play.

4
Laws of the Game

In the following pages the official laws of the game, approved by the International Football Association Board, are shown in shaded boxes.

Reproduction authorised by FIFA.

All rights reserved by FIFA.

Notes on the Laws of the Game

Modifications

Subject to the agreement of the national association concerned and provided the principles of these Laws are maintained, the Laws may be modified in their application for matches for players of under 16 years of age, for women footballers and for veteran footballers (over 35 years).

Any or all of the following modifications are permissible:

● *size of the field of play;*
● *size, weight and material of the ball;*
● *width between the goal-posts and height of the crossbar from the ground;*
● *the duration of the periods of play;*
● *number of substitutions.*

Further modifications are only allowed with the consent of the International Football Association Board.

Male and Female

References to the male gender in the Laws of the Game in respect of referees, assistant referees, players and officials are for simplification and apply to both males and females.

Key

Throughout the Laws of the Game the following symbol is used *

* Unless covered by the Special Circumstances listed in Law 8 - The Start and Restart of Play

5
Components

1   - **The Field of Play**
2   - **The Ball**
3   - **The Number of Players**
4   - **The Players' Equipment**

Players, ball, space
Players, ball and space are the three essential elements of every soccer game. For organised matches the first four laws prescribe the detail of each element.

Law 1 - The Field of Play
This is the stage upon which all soccer artists perform their skills. Both teams have equal territory to defend on a field large enough to provide ample space for twenty-two players and yet not too large to demand excessive physical effort.

While the areas marked within the boundary lines have fixed sizes there is much latitude allowed in the length and breadth. This is particularly useful where playing areas are restricted, e.g. public parks. More fields can be accommodated giving more people the opportunity to play the game.

The goal lines are self-explanatory, being where the goals are placed, but why are the sidelines named "touch lines"? The name is a survivor from the original laws of 1863. When the ball crossed the side boundary line the first player to "touch" the ball was then entitled to kick or throw it back into play.

Every soccer field must be longer than it is wide because an oblong-shape channels the flow of play between the two target goals. This

Why the law requires corner-posts to be a minimum of 5 feet (1.50 metres).

simple requirement contributes towards the interest and enjoyment of the game.

Safety factors for the players include a minimum height of 5 feet for the flagpost with a non-pointed top. V-shaped rut markings, which could easily cause injuries to ankles and legs, are not permitted.

Flagposts at the halfway line are optional, being a legacy from original laws which did not require a halfway line. They are, however, compulsory at the corners to help decide whether the ball has crossed the goal line or touch line.

The World Cup Final in 1974, between West Germany and Holland, nearly started without corner posts. The English referee, Jack Taylor, was about to blow his whistle when he realised that the posts had not been replaced after the field had been used for the pre-match ceremony. His alertness avoided an embarrassing incident.

Field markings need not be of a special colour - just distinctive. For important matches, particularly those shown on TV, we have become

Nets optional

○ **Penalty mark**

Goal and goal-area.

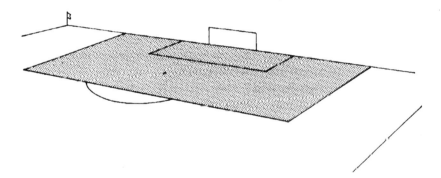

Penalty area.

used to seeing white lines on beautifully manicured green-grassed fields but blue or red markings on a snow covered surface are quite acceptable.

Target goals are of a size which demands skill from attacking players to put a ball into them and from a goalkeeper to keep it out. Goal nets may be attached to the goals but they are not obligatory thus avoiding an additional financial burden on many thousands of amateur clubs.

The Goal Area is the area from which goal kicks are taken.

The Penalty Area is a vital zone for two reasons. The goalkeeper is the only player allowed to handle the ball within its boundaries, subject to certain restraints described later, and all defending players must be careful to avoid committing certain offences which can result in a severe punishment - a Penalty kick - with a 90% chance of a goal being scored.

An arc, added to the penalty area, serves to mark a 10 yards (9.15 metres) distance from the penalty mark which must be observed by players as is explained in the penalty kick law (Law 14).

The centre circle serves the same purpose, at a kick off, where opponents must remain outside of the circle until the ball is kicked into play (Law 8). Another 10 yards reference mark may be added to the goal line, from the corner arc, to distance defending players at corner kicks (Law 17).

When the ball crosses a boundary line play stops and is restarted by a Throw-in (Law 15), a Goal Kick (Law 16) or a Corner Kick (Law 17).

Wisely the law does not specify the surface on which soccer is played. The choice is unlimited although unwritten considerations are that the chosen surface does not present undue danger to the players and that the game is not brought into disrepute by being played on a surface which denies skilful play, e.g. on a waterlogged or ice-covered field.

It is one of the duties of the referee to inspect the field and equipment before every game in good time to have any faulty items corrected.

Although not mentioned in soccer law the welfare and security of spectators must be considered particularly where large numbers are expected. Such matters concern possible risk of encroachment onto the field to interfere with play or to escape from incidents off the field. For top professional matches referees are instructed to inspect the area surrounding the field including exits, fences, etc.

Several tragic incidents, which have occurred in a number of countries, have imposed these precautions and placed an onerous responsibility on administrators, team officials, referees, players and spectators.

Law 1 - The Field of Play

Dimensions

The field of play must be rectangular. The length of the touch line must be greater than the length of the goal line.

Length: minimum 90 m
           (100 yds)
           maximum 120 m
           (130 yds)
Width: minimum 45 m
           (50 yds)
           maximum 90 m
           (100 yds)

International Matches

Length: minimum 100 m
           (110 yds)
           maximum 110 m
           (120 yds)
Width: minimum 64 m
           (70 yds)
           maximum 75 m
           (80 yds)

Field Markings

The field of play is marked with lines. These lines belong to the areas of which they are boundaries.

The two longer boundary lines are called touch lines. The two shorter lines are called goal lines.

All lines are not more than 12 cm (5 ins) wide.

The field of play is divided into two halves by a halfway line.

The centre mark is indicated at the midpoint of the halfway line. A circle with a radius of 9.15 m (10 yds) is marked around it.

The Goal Area

A goal area is defined at each end of the field as follows:

Two lines are drawn at right angles to the goal line, 5.5 m (6 yds) from the inside of each goalpost. These lines extend into the field of play for a distance of 5.5 m (6 yds) and are joined by a line drawn parallel with the goal line. The area bounded by these lines and the goal line is the goal area.

The Penalty Area

A penalty area is defined at each end of the field as follows:

Two lines are drawn at right angles to the goal line, 16.5 m (18 yds) from the inside of each goalpost. These lines extend into the field of play for a distance of 16.5 m (18 yds) and are joined by a line drawn parallel with the goal line. The area bounded by these lines and the goal line is the penalty area.

Within each penalty area a penalty mark is made 11 m (12 yds) from the midpoint between the goalposts and equidistant to them. An arc of a circle with a radius of 9.15 m (10 yds) from each penalty mark is drawn outside the penalty area.

Flagposts

A flagpost, not less than 1.5 m (5 ft) high, with a non-pointed top and a flag is placed at each corner.

Flagposts may also be placed at each end of the halfway line, not less than 1 m (1 yd) outside the touch line.

The Corner Arc

A quarter circle with a radius of 1 m (1 yd) from each corner flagpost is drawn inside the field of play.

Goals

Goals must be placed on the centre of each goal line.

They consist of two upright posts equidistant from the corner flagposts and joined at the top by a horizontal crossbar.

The distance between the posts is 7.32 m (8 yds) and the distance from the lower edge of the crossbar to the ground is 2.44 m (8 ft).

Both goalposts and the crossbar have the same width and depth which do not exceed 12 cm (5 ins). The goal lines are the same width as that of the goalposts and the crossbar. Nets may be attached to the goals and the ground behind the goal, provided that they are properly supported and do not interfere with the goalkeeper.

The goalposts and crossbars must be white.

Safety

Goals must be anchored securely to the ground. Portable goals may only be used if they satisfy this requirement.

Corner Flagpost

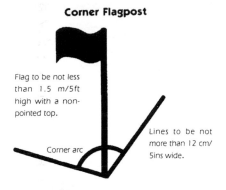

Flag to be not less than 1.5 m/5ft high with a non-pointed top.

Lines to be not more than 12 cm/5ins wide.

Corner arc

Decisions of the International FA. Board

● Decision 1

If the crossbar becomes displaced or broken, play is stopped until it has been repaired or replaced in position. If a repair is not possible, the match is abandoned. The use of a rope to replace the crossbar is not permitted. If the crossbar can be repaired, the match is restarted with a dropped ball at the place where the ball was located when play was stopped. (See Law 8)*

● Decision 2

Goalposts and crossbars must be made of wood, metal or other approved material. Their shape may be square, rectangular, round or elliptical and they must not be dangerous to players.

● Decision 3

No kind of commercial advertising, whether real or virtual, is permitted on the field of play and field equipment (including the goal nets and the areas they enclose) from the time the teams enter the field of play until they have left it at half-time and from the time the teams re-enter the field of play until the end of the match. In particular, no advertising material of any kind may be displayed on goals, nets, flagposts or their flags. No extraneous equipment (cameras, microphones, etc.) may be attached to these items.

● Decision 4

The reproduction, whether real or virtual, of representative logos or emblems of FIFA, confederations, national associations, leagues, clubs or other bodies, is forbidden on the field of play and field equipment (including the goal nets and the areas they enclose) during playing time, as described in Decision 3.

● Decision 5

A mark may be made off the field of play, 9.15 metres (10 yds) from the corner arc and at right angles to the goal lines to ensure that this distance is observed when a corner kick is being taken.

The Field of Play

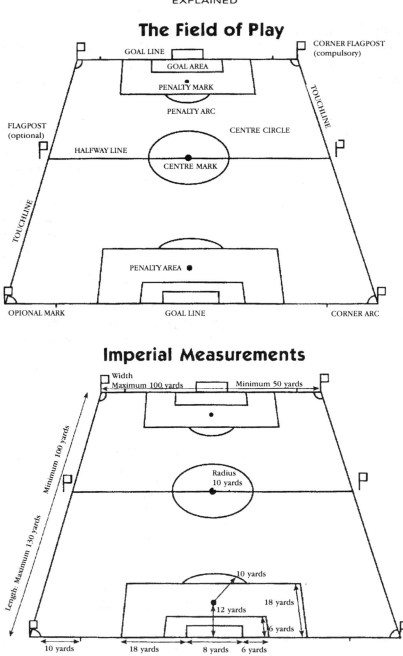

Imperial Measurements

Law 2 - The Ball

The ball is the heart of the game, the "magic" spherical object which reveals the abilities of players by reproducing and measuring their skills. It is about the size of a man's head, made from "safe" materials, inflated to a pressure which allows for variations in altitude and methods of manufacture, and not too heavy to be dangerous.

Modern soccer balls are high technology products made to official standards of quality. Selecting the match ball does not need to be a precise science. It should simply be suited to the conditions of play.

A hard ball is difficult to control on a hard surface because of excessive bounce causing errors of judgement, dangerous play, more ball-to-hand contact, more out-of-play stoppages, all adding up to frustration and consequent loss of enjoyment. A soft ball on a wet or muddy surface becomes a dull object with uncertain bounce, little roll, less vitality, less interest, all affecting the potential for enjoying the game.

Referees can avoid these problems by testing the match ball on the field before the game - in good time to adjust the ball pressure if necessary. A sound general rule to follow is - hard ground/soft ball : soft ground/hard ball.

A hard ball on a hard surface causes frustration and loss of enjoyment.

The ball may only be changed with the consent of the referee. In some matches several reserve balls are placed around the field with the object of replacing the match ball quickly should it leave the immediate area of the field. This is acceptable provided that the referee is satisfied that a replacement ball meets the requirements of the law.

The ball can burst or become deflated. Rare, but this phenomenon occurred in consecutive FA Cup Finals with the added curiosity that one club played in both matches. They were in 1946, Charlton Athletic v Derby County, and 1947, Charlton v Burnley.

The Law states how play is restarted after a ball becomes defective.

Law 2 - The Ball

Qualities and Measurements
The ball is:

- *spherical*
- *made of leather or other suitable material*
- *of a circumference of not more than 70 cm (28 ins) and not less than 68 cm (27 ins)*
- *not more than 450 g (16 oz) in weight and less than 410 g (14 oz) at the start of the match*
- *of a pressure equal to 0.6 - 1.1 atmosphere (600 - 1100g/cm²) at sea level (8.5 lbs/sq in 15.6 lbs/sq in)*

Replacement of a Defective Ball
If the ball bursts or becomes defective during the course of a match:

- *the match is stopped*
- *the match is restarted by dropping the replacement ball at the place where the first ball became defective* (see Law 8)*

If the ball bursts or becomes defective whilst not in play at a kick off, goal kick, corner kick, free kick, penalty kick or throw-in:

- *the match is restarted accordingly*

The ball may not be changed during the match without the authority of the referee.

Decisions of the International F.A. Board

● Decision 1

In competition matches, only footballs which meet the minimum technical requirements stipulated in Law 2 are permitted for use.

In FIFA competition matches, and in competition matches organised under the auspices of the confederations, acceptance of a football for use is conditional upon the football bearing one of the following three designations:

the official "FIFA APPROVED" logo,

or

the official "FIFA INSPECTED" logo,

or

the reference "INTERNATIONAL MATCHBALL STANDARD"

Such a designation on a football indicates that it has been tested officially and found to be in compliance with specific technical requirements, different for each category and additional to the minimum specifications stipulated in Law 2. The list of the additional requirements specific to each of the respective categories must be approved by the International F.A. Board. The institutes conducting the tests are subject to the approval of FIFA.

National association competitions may require the use of balls bearing any one of these three designations.

In all other matches the ball used must satisfy the requirements of Law 2.

● Decision 2

In FIFA competition matches and in competition matches organised under the auspices of the confederations and national associations, no kind of commercial advertising on the ball is permitted, except for the emblem of the competition, the competition organiser and the authorised trademark of the manufacturer. The competition regulations may restrict the size and number of such markings.

Recognised ball designations for FIFA competition matches.

Law 3 - The Number of Players

Although early laws made no mention of the number of players it was the practice for heads of teams to agree to eleven-a-side games. The practice was first recognised in the rules of the FA Challenge Cup, founded in 1871, and later incorporated into the laws.

One player must be designated as a goalkeeper but his role is not defined. The original definition read, "a goalkeeper is the defender who, for the time being, is nearest to his own goal" and "shall be at liberty to use his hands for the protection of his goal". At that time all players were dressed alike so the goalkeeper was identified by personal characteristics, such as a beard, although some wore a cap which aided recognition. Nowadays, goalkeepers wear colours different from the other players.

The "liberty" of using hands was generous because it applied to the whole of the defending team's half of the field. In the laws of 1912 this privilege was reduced to the penalty area and has remained so.

The role of the goalkeeper developed from the single task of preventing the ball from passing through the goal to that of a specialist with much influence on team tactics. In recent years the handling privilege became abused leading to unreasonable possession of the ball, delaying tactics and undue emphasis on negative defensive play. In Law 12 we shall see how restrictions have been imposed on the goalkeeper with the intention of encouraging attacking play.

Interestingly, the law does not mention the actual positions of players. It is obvious that the goalkeeper will position himself near to his goal to take advantage of his handling privilege but he is not prevented from moving to any part of the field. Some modern goalkeepers create interest and excitement by leaving the penalty area for sorties towards the opponents' goal. The Colombian goalkeeper, José René Higuita, was one of the first to demonstrate this tactic during the 1990 World Cup matches in Italy.

Any player may change places with the goalkeeper during a normal stoppage in play and provided that the referee is notified.

As for the "outfield" players the law wisely says nothing, allowing complete freedom for team managers to devise tactics which combine individual skills in the best interest of team play. The diagrams on page 55 illustrate two modern tactical formations.

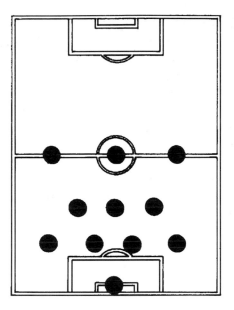

The 4-3-3 system.

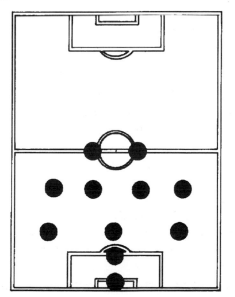

The "sweeper" system with 3-4-2. No fixed formation of players. These are just two of several combinations with specific tasks in defence, mid-field and attack.

About 95% of the text of this law deals with substitutions of any of the basic team of eleven allowing up to three in official competition matches and not more than five in other matches.

Substitutes were originally permitted when players were injured, in order to maintain numerical equality, but not in competition matches. There was a reluctance to allow substitutions in all matches because it was thought that the character of the game would suffer. Television had an influence on a change of view when millions of fans saw several important matches, such as FA Cup Finals, spoiled by the spectacle of injured players continuing under obvious stress.

The law does not restrict substitutions to injured players but the spirit behind this concession remains despite the frequent use of replacements for tactical reasons.

The procedure for a substitution is:

a. there is a normal stoppage in the game;
b. the referee is notified;
c. the outgoing player has left the field;
d. the referee signals permission for the new player to enter the field;
e. the new player enters at the halfway line.

Replaced players take no further part in the game. This prevents the reuse of a player considered to have been injured seriously enough to be substituted and restricts an extension of tactical substitutions.

The minimum number of players in a team may be fixed by National Associations although the International Board recommend a minimum of seven.

Players must obtain the permission of the referee to enter or leave the field. All substitutes are subject to the authority and jurisdiction of the referee whether called upon to play or not. They are members of the team and may be disciplined for any misconduct reported by the referee.

Procedure for substitutions.

Eleven World Champions. The Brazilian team, winners of the 1994 World Cup.
Photo: Peter Robinson.

Law 3 - The Number of Players

Players

A match is played by two teams, each consisting of not more than eleven players, one of whom is the goalkeeper. A match may not start if either team consists of fewer than seven players.

Official Competitions

Up to a maximum of three substitutes may be used in any match played in an official competition organised under the auspices of FIFA, the confederations or the national associations.

The rules of the competition must state how many substitutes may be nominated, from three up to a maximum of seven.

Other Matches

In other matches, up to five substitutes may be used, provided that:

- *the teams concerned reach agreement on a maximum number*
- *the referee is informed before the match*

If the referee is not informed, or if no agreement is reached before the start of the match, no more than three substitutes are allowed.

All Matches

In all matches the names of the substitutes must be given to the referee prior to the start of the match. Substitutes not so named may not take part in the match.

Substitution Procedure

To replace a player by a substitute, the following conditions must be observed:

- *the referee is informed before any proposed substitution is made*
- *a substitute only enters the field of play after the player being replaced has left and after receiving a signal from the referee*
- *a substitute only enters the field of play at the halfway line and during a stoppage in the match*
- *a substitution is completed when a substitute enters the field of play*
- *from that moment, the substitute becomes a player and the player*

he has replaced ceases to be a player

● a player who has been replaced takes no further part in the match

● all substitutes are subject to the authority and jurisdiction of the referee, whether called upon to play or not

Changing the Goalkeeper

Any of the other players may change places with the goalkeeper, provided that:

● the referee is informed before the change is made

● the change is made during a stoppage in the match

Infringements/Sanctions

If a substitute enters the field of play without the referee's permission:

● play is stopped

● the substitute is cautioned, shown the yellow card and required to leave the field of play

● play is restarted with a dropped ball at the place it was located when play was stopped * (see Law 8)

If a player changes places with the goalkeeper without the referee's permission before the change is made:

● play continues

● the players concerned are cautioned and shown the yellow card when the ball is next out of play

For any other infringements of this Law:

● the players concerned are cautioned and shown the yellow card

Restart of Play

If play is stopped by the referee to administer a caution:

● the match is restarted by an indirect free kick, to be taken by a player of the opposing team from the place where the ball was located when play was stopped * (see Law 8)

Players and Substitutes Sent Off

A player who has been sent off before the kick off may be replaced only by one of the named substitutes.

A named substitute who has been sent off, either before the kick off or after play has started, may not be replaced.

Decisions of the International F.A. Board

● Decision 1

Subject to the overriding conditions of Law 3, the minimum number of players in a team is left to the discretion of national associations. The Board is of the opinion, however, that a match should not continue if there are fewer than seven players in either team.

● Decision 2

The coach may convey tactical instructions to the players during the match. He and the other officials must remain within the confines of the technical area, where such an area is provided, and they must behave in a responsible manner.

Law 4 - The Players' Equipment

Soccer is not a dangerous sport but there is a clear message in the first paragraph of this law for safety and protection. It spells out the responsibility of players to protect themselves from injury.

Most injuries in soccer affect the legs below the knees but, although shinguards have been worn since 1874 (invented by S. Widdowson) they were not made compulsory equipment until 1990.

Soccer boots, the most frequent cause of injury, were the subject of hundreds of words in this law before 1990. Detailed technical

Why shinguards are compulsory.

Shin protection - ancient shinguards over bare legs.

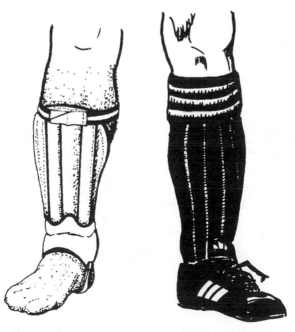

. . . and modern. Shinguards must be covered entirely by stockings.

specifications, intended mainly for manufacturers and to guide referees, regulated the shapes, sizes, materials, and numbers of studs and bars. Now, soccer footwear is just one of the elements of the all-embracing directive in the first words of this law.

This emphasises the responsibility of the player to choose footwear with great care and to ensure that the element of danger, inherent in studs and bars, is kept within reason. Hard surfaces will quickly wear studs to sharp edges. Soft surfaces will tempt players to fit extra long studs.

Watches, rings, pendants, solid plaster casts, leg supports, and even some goalkeepers' gloves, are elements of danger which can be avoided.

Referees have a clear duty to inspect players' equipment before every match in good time to allow adjustments to be completed. To underline the point the whole world was kept waiting for the start of the 1978 World Cup Final, between Argentina and Holland, when the Dutch player Van de Kerkhof appeared on the field wearing a plaster cast on a hand. Argentine players protested to the referee who was obliged to allow several minutes for the cast to be covered. The incident created much bad feeling which could have been avoided.

Law 4 - The Players' Equipment

Safety
A player must not use equipment or wear anything which is dangerous to himself or another player (including any kind of jewellery).

Basic Equipment
The basic compulsory equipment of a player is:

- *a jersey or shirt*

- *shorts - if thermal undershorts are worn, they are of the same main colour as the shorts*
- *stockings*
- *shinguards*
- *footwear*

Shinguards
- *are covered entirely by the stockings*
- *are made of a suitable material*

(rubber, plastic or similar substances)

● provide a reasonable degree of protection

Goalkeepers

● each goalkeeper wears colours which distinguish him from the other players, the referee and the assistant referees

Infringements/Sanctions

For any infringement of this Law:

● play need not be stopped

● the player at fault is instructed by the referee to leave the field of play to correct his equipment

● the player leaves the field of play when the ball next ceases to be in play, unless he has already corrected his equipment

● any player required to leave the field of play to correct his equipment does not re-enter without the referee's permission

● the referee checks that the player's equipment is correct before allowing him to re-enter the field of play

● the player is only allowed to re-enter the field of play when the ball is out of play

A player who has been required to leave the field of play because of an infringement of this Law and who enters (or re-enters) the field of play without the referee's permission is cautioned and shown the yellow card.

Restart of Play

If play is stopped by the referee to administer a caution:

● the match is restarted by an indirect free kick taken by a player of the opposing side, from the place where the ball was located when the referee stopped the match* (see Law 8)

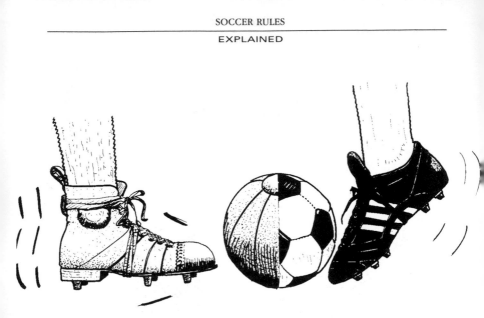

Steel toe-caps were needed in heavy boots to punt a heavy leather ball.
Today lightweight shoes help players to caress the modern-style ball with greater accuracy and pace.

6
Control

Law 5 - The Referee
Law 6 - The Assistant Referees

Referees and Assistant Referees

Many soccer games are played without qualified referees and assistants because there is a shortage of officials in relation to the demand. A game cannot be played to its full potential unless a neutral person is available to decide points of contention promptly and to guide the play within the framework of the laws. The match officials contribute much to the enjoyment of players and spectators by interfering as little as is necessary to maintain control and ensure that fair play is observed.

Laws 5 and 6 describe the duties and responsibilities of match officials and the exceptional authority delegated to them by the administrators of the game.

The referee arrives in the nick of time. Photo: FIFA

Law 5 - The Referee

Definition: "Referee: One to whom a matter in dispute is referred for decision."

Applied to the role of the soccer referee this definition was appropriate in the last century when the referee, a neutral person, waited on the touch line for appeals for decisions from two umpires, appointed by the teams, standing in the field of play. His role was passive and remained so until 1891 when a mounting frequency of disputes caused many interruptions in play. To enforce the laws promptly and more efficiently the referee was transferred into the game while the umpires moved to the touchlines to become linesmen.

The original function of the referee, "to decide disputed points", appeared in the laws until 1973 when it was finally recognised that his duties and responsibilities had evolved to cover all aspects of an organised game.

Today, the principal match official is, effectively, a superintendent of play. The definition:

"Superintendent: One who manages and directs; has charge and oversight of an activity; controls with authority."

is more appropriate and sums up the job specification of the referee detailed in Law 5.

It amounts to total power to supervise, manage, direct and control the conduct of a soccer game.

Only referees know the enormous amount of time devoted to studying the meaning and practical interpretation of the fine print of every law. Every referee is required to be a trained expert, to attend regular courses, seminars, discussion groups, absorb advice from senior colleagues and apply this knowledge on the field by recognising instantly any infringement and then to impose the correct discipline with firmness and dignity.

From the foregoing summary it is clear that a dedicated referee is a person with a deep passion for the game, well trained in theory and practice and having the courage to make instant decisions, however unpopular they may be. Add another essential requirement, a physical condition equivalent to an athlete, and we are describing a very special person in soccer, a person to be saluted for an exceptional contribution to the well-being of our favourite sport.

Advantage

Further proof of the extraordinary powers granted to the referee is that the "advantage clause" allows him to set aside the written law and apply a personal interpretation of fair play by not stopping play for an offence if, in his opinion, the team offended against would benefit from this decision.

An obvious example would be where an attacker is tripped but, before the referee stops play, he is able to continue with a good chance of scoring a goal. The referee allows play to proceed with a call of "advantage" and a signal to play on. Another example: a defender handles the ball just before it goes into the goal. Law 12 requires a penalty kick to be awarded but the offending team would benefit if the penalty kick was not converted. The referee would allow the goal.

The referee will sometimes allow a free kick to be taken quickly before opposing players have observed the 10 yards limit, required by Law 13, considering that delay would be to the advantage of the offending team.

When should advantage be applied? So much depends on the attitude and sportsmanship of the players as to whether the game can be allowed to flow or requires constant checking for rough or illegal play. Generally, referees are advised to exercise caution in the first few minutes in order to establish clear authority.

Advantage should always be allowed when a goal is almost certain but not in cases of serious misconduct or injury. Clear communication of advantage is important. Situations arise where an offence has been seen by the players and spectators but, in the opinion of the referee, play should continue. If the referee's thinking is not clearly understood it is often concluded that either the official missed the offence or considered that it was not an offence. The official may have made an excellent decision but poor communication invites criticism to the detriment of his authority and pleasure of the game.

Clear communication of referees' decisions is of concern to all. Not only should the players be aware of the reasons for stopping play but also, as the sport has such a wide spectator appeal, those who watch should be helped to understand the cause and effect of match incidents. See the Introduction to this book.

Studies have shown that referees want to communicate their decisions and do so by simple, instinctive gestures, e.g. touching an arm to indicate a handling offence, raising a foot to mime a dangerous kick, etc. The laws require only one signal from the referee - to raise one arm to signify that a free kick is indirect (Law 13). Other approved signals are illustrated on pages 80-88.

The referee is required to keep the game moving by interfering as little as possible, dealing firmly with clear breaches of the laws and stopping play for a seriously injured player to be removed for treatment. Other less serious injuries can be dealt with on the touch

Advantage. A foul has been committed here but play is allowed to continue as there is a good chance of a goal being scored.

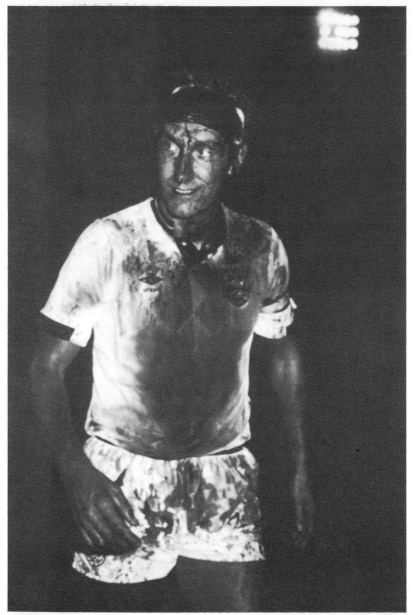

A sight which should never again be seen on a soccer field. Referees are directed to insist that badly injured players should leave the field for adequate treatment. Photo: Bob Thomas.

line. In cases of doubt the referee may allow a team official (preferably a medical person) to enter the field and to examine the player but not to carry out treatment. In some countries the referee displays a green card to confirm that an official may enter the field.

Recent alarms over the transmission of serious diseases, via blood spilled at sports injuries, moved the International Board to insist, in this law, that ". . . any player bleeding from a wound leaves the field of play".

The referee has total command over who enters or leaves the field and to stop, suspend or abandon a game where the elements, interference by spectators, or any other cause, makes such action necessary. Apart from the formal duties and responsibilities prescribed for controlling on-the-field action the modern referee must be concerned with supervising off-the-field coaching. Since 1993 team coaches have had the right to convey tactical instructions to players during a match. This was a major departure from the fundamental principle, held sacred for 130 years, that players be allowed freedom to solve problems in their own way.

Rigid and aggressive coaching stifles spontaneity, causes irritation, frustration and incitement to misconduct. It also affects the dignity of the game.

The referee is therefore concerned to ensure that coaching is contained within reasonable bounds.

Where large audiences may be present at a match the referee is required to consider the welfare of all concerned by consulting with

Rigid and aggressive coaching during play can stifle spontaneity, cause irritation and frustration to players.

security authorities and those in charge of law and order.

Referees who have charge of matches at national and international levels have travelled a long road, serving an apprenticeship for several years in junior and senior amateur soccer. They are all human and can make errors but, as a neutral official, the referee's decision must always be accepted as final even when it may be seen to be wrong. Self-discipline is, after all, one of the qualities of character fundamental to the well-being of the individual and the sport.

Law 5 - The Referee

The Authority of the Referee

Each match is controlled by a referee who has full authority to enforce the Laws of the Game in connection with the match to which he has been appointed.

Powers and Duties

The Referee:

- *enforces the laws of the Game*
- *controls the match in co-operation with the assistant referees and, where applicable, with the fourth official*
- *ensures that the ball meets the requirements of Law 2*
- *ensures that the players' equipment meets the requirement of Law 4*
- *acts as timekeeper and keeps a record of the match*
- *stops, suspends or terminates the match, at his discretion, for any infringements of the Laws*

- *stops, suspends or terminates the match, because of outside interference of any kind*
- *stops the match if, in his opinion, a player is seriously injured and ensures that he is removed from the field of play*
- *allows play to continue until the ball is out of play if a player is, in his opinion, only slightly injured*
- *ensures that any player bleeding from a wound leaves the field of play. The player may only return on receiving a signal from the referee, who must be satisfied that the bleeding has stopped*
- *allows play to continue when the team against which an offence has been committed will benefit from such an advantage and penalises the original offence if the anticipated advantage does not ensue at that time*

- *punishes the more serious offence when a player commits more than one offence at the same time*
- *takes disciplinary action against players guilty of cautionable and sending-off offences. He is not obliged to take this action immediately but must do so when the ball next goes out of play*
- *takes action against team officials who fail to conduct themselves in a responsible manner and may at his discretion, expel them from the field of play and its immediate surrounds*
- *acts on the advice of assistant referees regarding incidents which he has not seen*
- *ensures that no unauthorised persons enter the field of play*

- *restarts the match after it has been stopped*
- *provides the appropriate authorities with a match report which includes information on any disciplinary action taken against players, and/or team officials and any other incidents which occurred before, during or after the match*

Decisions of the Referee

The decisions of the referee regarding facts connected with play are final.

The referee may only change a decision on realising that it is incorrect or, at his discretion, on the advice of an assistant referee, provided that he has not restarted play.

Decisions of the International F.A. Board

● Decision 1

A referee (or where applicable, an assistant referee or fourth official) is not held liable for:

any kind of injury suffered by a player, official or spectator

any damage to property of any kind

any other loss suffered by any individual, club, company, association or other body, which is due or which may be due to any decision which he may take under the terms of the Laws of the Game or in respect of the normal procedures required to hold, play and control a match.

This may include:

- *a decision that the condition of the field of play or its surrounds or that the weather conditions are such as to allow or not to allow a match to take place*
- *a decision to abandon a match for whatever reason*
- *a decision as to the condition of the fixtures or equipment used during a match including the goalposts, crossbar, flagposts and the ball*
- *a decision to stop or not to stop a match due to spectator interference or any problem in the spectator area*
- *a decision to stop or not to stop play to allow an injured player to be removed from the field of play for treatment*
- *a decision to request or insist that an injured player be removed from the field of play for treatment*
- *a decision to allow or not to allow a player to wear certain apparel or equipment*
- *a decision (in so far as this may be his responsibility) to allow or not to allow any persons (including team or stadium officials, security officers, photographers or other media representatives) to be present in the vicinity of the field of play*
- *any other decision which he takes in accordance with the Laws of the Game or in conformity with his duties under the terms of FIFA, confederation, national association or league rules or regulations under which the match is played*

● **Decision 2**

In tournaments or competitions where a fourth official is appointed, his role and duties must be in accordance with the guidelines approved by the International F.A. Board.

Referees in action. Photo: Pro-Sport.

Signals by the Referee and Assistant Referees

The signals illustrated in this memorandum have been approved by the International F.A. Board for use by registered referees of affiliated National Associations. Illustrations concerning signals by the referee are shown on pages 80-88. They are simple, universally in use and well understood.

While it is not the duty of the referee to explain or mime any offence that has caused him to give a particular decision, there are times when a simple gesture or word of guidance can aid communication and assist toward greater understanding, and gaining more respect, to the mutual benefit of referee and players. Improving communication should be encouraged, but the exaggerated miming of offences can be undignified and confusing and should not be used.

An indication by the referee of the point where a throw-in should be taken may well help prevent a player from taking a throw-in improperly. A call of "Play on, advantage" confirms to a player that the referee has not simply missed a foul, but has chosen to apply advantage. Even an indication that the ball was minutely deflected by its touching another player on its path across a touch-line might be helpful too in generating a greater understanding between referee and players. A better understanding will lead to more harmonious relationships.

All signals given by the referee should be simple, clear and instinctive. They should be designed to control the game efficiently and to ensure continuous play as far as possible; they are intended essentially to indicate what the next action in the game should be, not principally to justify that action.

An arm pointing to indicate a corner-kick, goal-kick or foul, and the direction in which it is to be taken, will normally be sufficient. The raised arm to indicate that a free-kick is indirect is clearly understood, but if a player queries politely whether the award is a direct free-kick or an indirect freekick, a helpful word from the referee, in addition to the regular signal, will lead to a better understanding in future.

The proper use of the whistle, voice and hand signals by the referee and the flags by the linesmen should all assist understanding through clear communication.

Direct free kick
The hand and arm clearly indicate the direction.

Indirect free kick
This signal shall be maintained until the kick has been taken and retained until the ball has been played or touched by another player or goes out of play.

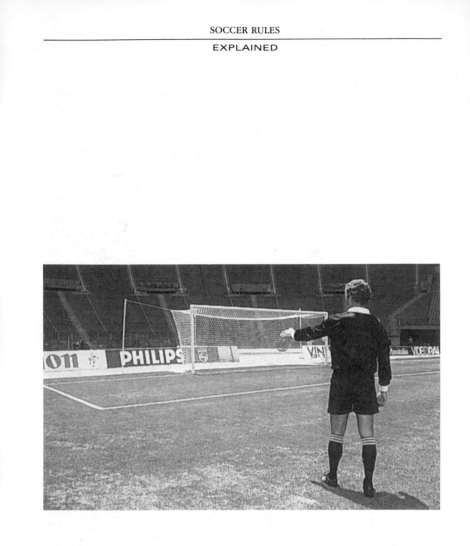

Goal kick

Goal kick

Play on - advantage
Where the referee see an offence but uses the "advantage", he shall indicate that play shall continue

Caution or expulsion

With the card system, the card shall be shown in the manner illustrated. The player's identity must be recorded at the time.

Corner kick

Penalty kick
The referee clearly indicates the penalty mark, but there is no need to run towards it.

Law 6 - The Assistant Referees

Referees rely heavily on neutral assistants who are qualified referees in their own right and are controlling matches in the middle when not doing duty on the touchline. Effectively three qualified officials supervise the play.

In addition to the obvious assistance of signalling the ball out of play, which side is entitled to restart the game and when a substitution is required (as shown on pages 92-99), neutral assistants help the referee before the game starts with inspections of the field and equipment. They keep a check on timing of play, are expected to call the attention of the referee to rough play or misconduct, give advice on any point put to them by the referee and generally assist in conducting the game in accordance with the laws.

Their signals are essentially for the information of the referee. Players should not stop when a flag is raised but play to the referee's whistle. The referee may have seen the incident from a better angle or may decide to use advantage.

When neutral officials are not available each team is expected to appoint a club official to assist on the touchline. Their duties are usually restricted to signalling when the ball crosses a boundary line and indicating which team should restart play. However, other duties may be delegated by the referee but he has the ultimate responsibility for all decisions.

It is a fact that not all good referees make good assistants. Studies of World Cup tournaments have shown up serious deficiencies among top referees when given an assistant's role. FIFA decided in 1990 to create a special panel of assistant referees for international matches.

Law 6 - The Assistant Referees

Duties
Two assistant referees are appointed whose duties, subject to the decision of the referee, are to indicate:

● *when the whole of the ball has passed out of the field of play*
● *which side is entitled to a corner kick, goal kick or throw-in*
● *when a player may be penalised for being in an offside position*
● *when a substitution is requested*

● *when misconduct or any other incident has occurred out of the view of the referee*

Assistance
The assistant referees also assist the referee to control the match in accordance with the Laws of the Game.

In the event of undue interference or improper conduct, the referee will relieve an assistant referee of his duties and make a report to the appropriate authorities.

Control
Co-operation between match officials
Additional official notes on Laws 5 and 6

The referee operates the diagonal system of control if his assistant referees are neutral. If they are not neutral he informs them which method he intends to use. He co-operates with his assistant referees on the following matters and tells them:

(a) *the time by his watch;*

(b) *the side of the field which each assistant referee shall take in each half of the match;*

(c) *their duties prior to the start of the game, such as checking field equipment;*

(d) *who shall be the senior assistant referee;*

(e) *their positioning during corner-kicks;*

(f) *the sign denoting that he has noticed his assistant referee's signal but has overruled it;*

(g) *which detail in the throw-in shall be observed by the assistant referee and which by the referee. Some referees ask their assistant referees to watch out for foot faults while they themselves concentrate on hand faults.*

Referees do not necessarily keep to one diagonal of the field of play. If the state of the ground or the weather demands a switch to the opposite diagonal, the referee indicates his intention to make such a change-over to the assistant referees, who move to the other half of their line. One advantage of such a change in diagonal is that the surface of the ground next to the touch-line will be less worn out because the whole length of the field will be utilised.

Other methods of co-operation may be used as long as all three officials are aware of them.

Offside
Flag held upright to indicate offside.

Offside
When the referee stops play, the signal indicates position on far side of the field.

Offside
Position near the centre of the field.

Offside
Position on or near side of the field.

Substitution
Front view of the signal to the referee when a substitution is requested.

Throw-in

Goal kick

Corner kick

The assistant referee should signal that the ball has gone out of play. He should also look at the referee in case he has already made his own decision which may be different from the assistant's.

7
Game Rules

Basic procedures

As in any other sport this group of laws outlines basic procedure for the duration of play, how to start a game, when the ball is in or out of play and method of scoring.

Law 7 - The Duration of the Match

The normal duration of a match has stood the test of time since the mid-1880s. Divided into two 45-minute periods, with a compulsory break at half-time, players have a reasonable time to demonstrate individual and team skills without exhaustion.

There are exceptions. Teams may agree to play a friendly match to last as long as they wish and a shorter duration is allowed for under-16-year-olds, veteran and women players. Some competitions may have a special rule requiring teams to play extra-time, usually two periods of 15 minutes, to try and achieve a definite result.

The actual time that the ball is in play varies from game to game. The official FIFA Statistics covering the 52 matches played in the 1994 World Cup record an average of 61 minutes. The longest and shortest times were 70 minutes and 56 minutes respectively. Evidently each game has its own character. One match may flow easily whereas another may require many stoppages. In USA '94 stoppages ranged from a minimum of 83 to a maximum of 132!

For many years it has been common practice for the referee to make no allowance for time taken up during routine stoppages, e.g. when the ball goes out of play over the touch or goal lines. However, recent trends in the game have led to an unacceptable loss of ball-in-play time. Deliberate time-wasting tactics, more frequent use of substitutions and greater concern for injured players have persuaded the International Board to tighten up this law and to instruct referees to be more strict in making due allowances.

How much time to allow is always at the discretion of the referee. He is the only recognised timekeeper and makes his judgements according to the circumstances in each game.

Every player has the right to an interval at half time, not exceeding 15 minutes.

The referee has no option but to extend time to allow a penalty kick to be completed if awarded at the end of the first or second periods. This was written into the law after an incident in a match played between Stoke City and Aston Villa in 1892. Stoke were awarded a penalty with just two minutes left for play. The Aston Villa goalkeeper kicked the ball far out of the playing area and it could not be found within the time remaining. The referee was obliged to end the game. Stoke lost 1-0 and the law was amended to correct what was clearly seen to be a situation against the spirit of fair play.

An uncompleted match must be replayed unless the rules of the competition concerned allow the result to stand or award the match to one of the teams.

The latter option was applied after an important World Cup qualifying match between Brazil and Chile played in Rio de Janeiro in 1989. After 69 minutes Brazil were leading 1-0 when the Chilean goalkeeper appeared to have been injured by a flare thrown onto the field by a fan. His injury seemed serious enough to the Chilean players to justify refusing to continue the match and to claim a replay on neutral territory.

FIFA's subsequent enquiry proved that the goalkeeper had not been injured but had taken part in an attempt to have the match abandoned. The match was awarded to Brazil, as a 2-0 victory. The goalkeeper, and several team officials, were severely punished for bringing the game into disrepute.

Law 7 - The Duration of the Match

Periods of Play

The match lasts two equal periods of 45 minutes, unless otherwise mutually agreed between the referee and the two participating teams. Any agreement to alter the periods of play (for example to reduce each half to 40 minutes because of insufficient light) must be made before the start of play and must comply with competition rules.

Half-Time Interval

Players are entitled to an interval at half-time.

The half-time interval must not exceed 15 minutes.

Competition rules must state the duration of the half-time interval.

The duration of the half-time interval may be altered only with the consent of the referee.

Allowance for Time Lost

Allowance is made in either period for all time lost through:

- *substitution(s)*
- *assessment of injury to players*
- *removal of injured players from the field of play for treatment*
- *wasting time*
- *any other cause*

The allowance for time lost is at the discretion of the referee.

Penalty Kick

Additional time is allowed for a penalty kick to be taken at the end of each half or at the end of periods of extra time.

Extra Time

Competition rules may provide for two further equal periods to be played. The conditions of Law 8 will apply.

Abandoned Match

An abandoned match is replayed unless the competition rules provide otherwise.

Law 8 - The Start and Restart of Play

The ceremony which takes place before a game starts can have an important influence on the result. After the referee has greeted the two captains a toss of a coin gives the winning captain the choice of goal to attack.

Is there any difference? An astute captain will have assessed the playing conditions, noting the immediate and possible influence of the sun, wind direction and strength, a sloping surface, etc. to decide which goal to attack. A "lucky" end or the end where his team's supporters are gathered may be factors in his decision.

The opposing team have first possession of the ball and start play with a kick off in the centre of the field. There are many examples of goals scored within a few seconds of the kick off to make this a potential match winner.

To encourage an immediate assault on the goal the IFAB changed the law, in 1997, to allow a goal to be scored DIRECT from a kick off - quite possible on short fields against a team with a sleepy goalkeeper!

A team conceding a goal is given possession of the ball for a kick off. An interesting early rule of Harrow School required teams to change ends after a goal was scored, or, "if no goal has been obtained by 3 o'clock" - an example of equalising playing conditions!

The team which does not have first possession at the start of play restarts with a kick off after the half-time interval.

There are rare occasions when a game is started by the referee dropping the ball between opposing players. This can occur anywhere on the field after the game has been stopped for a special reason, e.g. a serious injury or interference by an outside agency.

If extra periods of play are required the toss-up ceremony is repeated to decide choice of goal to attack.

Soccer law has such authority that a King, President, or any other person, is not allowed to start a match. The play must be decided by the players. A VIP is the equivalent of an outside agency.

If a special ceremony is arranged, for a charity or exhibition match, the ball may be kicked but it must be returned to the centre spot for a kick off prescribed in this law.

The kick off: opponents at least 10 yards from the ball. The ball must be kicked forward.

Law 8 - The Start and Restart of Play

Preliminaries

A coin is tossed and the team which wins the toss decides which goal it will attack in the first half of the match.

The other team takes the kick off to start the match.

The team which wins the toss takes the kick off to start the second half of the match.

In the second half of the match the teams change ends and attack the opposite goals.

Kick off

A kick off is a way of starting or restarting play:

- *at the start of the match*
- *after a goal has been scored*
- *at the start of the second half of the match*
- *at the start of each period of extra time, where applicable*

A goal may be scored directly from the kick off.

Procedure

- *all players are in their own half of the field*
- *the opponents of the team taking the kick off are at least 9.15 m (10 yds) from the ball until it is in play*
- *the ball is stationary on the centre mark*

- *the referee gives a signal*
- *the ball is in play when it is kicked and moves forward*
- *the kicker does not touch the ball a second time until it has touched another player*

After a team scores a goal, the kick off is taken by the other team.

Infringements/Sanctions

If the kicker touches the ball a second time before it has touched another player:

- *an indirect free kick is awarded to the opposing team to be taken from the place where the infringement occurred**

For any other infringement of the kick off procedure:

- *the kick off is retaken*

Dropped Ball

A dropped ball is a way of restarting the match after a temporary stoppage which becomes necessary, while the ball is in play, for any reason not mentioned elsewhere in the Laws of the Game.

Procedure

The referee drops the ball at the place where it was located when play was stopped.*

Play restarts when the ball touches the ground.

Infringements/Sanctions

The ball is dropped again:

- *if it is touched by a player before it makes contact with the ground*
- *if the ball leaves the field of play after it makes contact with the ground, without a player touching it*

*Special Circumstances

A free kick awarded to the defending team inside its own goal area is taken from any point within the goal area.

An indirect free kick awarded to the attacking team in its opponents' goal area is taken from the goal area line parallel to the goal line at the point nearest to where the infringement occurred.

A dropped ball to restart the match after play has been temporarily stopped inside the goal area takes place on the goal area line parallel to the goal line at the point nearest to where the ball was located when play was stopped.

Law 9 - The Ball In and Out of Play

From the kick off the ball is in play at all times until it crosses a boundary line or play is stopped by the referee.

The ball must "wholly cross" the boundary line. Whenever there is doubt, either for the ball being in or out of play, or, a possible infringement, the best advice for players is to "Play to the whistle".

Law 9 - The Ball In and Out of Play

Ball Out of Play

The ball is out of play when:

- *it has wholly crossed the goal line or touch line whether on the ground or in the air*
- *play has been stopped by the referee*

Ball In Play

The ball is in play at all other times, including when:

- *it rebounds from a goal post, crossbar or corner flagpost and remains in the field of play*
- *it rebounds from either the referee or an assistant referee when they are on the field of play*

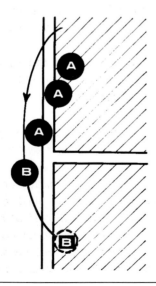

As are IN PLAY.
B is OUT OF PLAY.

Law 10 - The Method of Scoring

The main object of the game is to put the ball through the opponents' goal in a legal manner. Normally, goals are scored with a foot or the head but any part of the body may be used except an arm or a hand. It would be legal if a goalkeeper threw the ball from his own penalty area into the opponents' goal but the possibility is so rare as to be practically non-existent. There are, however, cases of goalkeepers kicking the ball into the other goal after handling it inside their own penalty area. Pat Jennings, goalkeeper for Tottenham Hotspur, accomplished this feat during the 1967 F.A. Charity Shield match against Manchester United.

On the same principle as Law 9, the whole of the ball must pass through the goal which means clearing the exterior edges of the goalposts because, in Law 1, the goal lines and goalposts must be of the same width.

If the ball wholly crosses the goal line between the posts but spins or rebounds into play a goal is scored. This can be difficult to judge with a fast moving ball and requires excellent positioning by the match officials. A goal which caused much controversy was England's third against West Germany in the 1966 World Cup Final. From Geoff Hurst's shot the ball struck the underside of the crossbar, dropped on or near the goal line and rebounded into play to be headed away by a defender.

England players claimed a goal but the Germans insisted that the ball had not crossed the goal line.

Was it a goal or not? Millions were kept waiting for the answer while the Swiss referee ran to the touch line to consult the Russian linesman. Although not ideally placed the linesman pointed to the centre of the field to signal a goal.

Photographs and films have not satisfactorily proved the validity of the goal but history records that it was a vital factor in the result of the match won by England 4-2.

Defenders make mistakes and sometimes score against their own team - "an own goal". Bert Turner had this misfortune playing for Charlton against Derby County during the 1946 FA Cup Final but, one minute later, he scored again, this time in the opponents' goal!

Referees have been known to "score" goals when the ball has been deflected from them into the goal. Such a goal is valid because the

NO

A goal is not scored until the ball has completely crossed the goal line between the posts. Credit: Pro Sport.

NO

YES

referee is a neutral agent, equivalent to a moving goalpost!

A goal cannot be scored from an Indirect free kick (Law 13), Throw-in (Law 15) or from a free kick awarded to the defending team. Nor can a goal be allowed if interference occurs from an outside agent such as a spectator, animal or an object.

Nowadays, each goal is recorded by the referee in a notebook but an ancient practice was to "score" a notch in a goalpost! Effectively, players win goals but it is the referee who scores them!

Law 10 - The Method of Scoring

Goal Scored

A goal is scored when the whole of the ball passes over the goal line, between the goalposts and under the crossbar, provided that no infringement of the Laws of the Game has been committed previously by the team scoring the goal.

Winning Team

The team scoring the greater number of goals during a match is the winner. If both teams score an equal number of goals, or if no goals are scored, the match is drawn.

Competition Rules

For matches ending in a draw, competition rules may state provisions involving extra time, or other procedures approved by the International F.A. Board to determine the winner of a match.

England's controversial third goal against West Germany in the 1966 World Cup Final at Wembley. Did the whole of the ball cross the line? Photo: The Football Association.

8
Technical
Law 11 - Offside

The offside law is a technical law because it relates to tactical play while the ball is in motion. As will be seen from the extensive commentary on this law, there is a sound reason for an offside rule in soccer and other team games. It involves fair play, discipline, tactical innovation, skill and enjoyment.

When the basic elements are understood it is not difficult to follow how the law applies in practice. Players can improve their own and team performances when they know how to avoid offside.

Law 11 - Offside

Offside is the least understood and the most controversial law in soccer. It need not be as the following comments will attempt to explain.

The number of offsides in a match can vary from zero (Italy v Poland 1982 World Cup) to as many as 22 (England v Kuwait '82 WC). The average in the USA94 World Cup was 6.

Why is offside necessary in soccer? A tactical law, it is concerned with the position of players when the ball is in play. Its purpose is evident from a brief look at its origin and development.

Offside can be related to the game of "harpastum", a form of mock battle played by Roman soldiers nearly 2000 years ago as part of military training exercises. Equal forces were assembled to contest the game on a limited area. The object was to capture an enemy stronghold by moving a ball, about the size of a man's head, to and behind the opponents' base line. In so doing the soldiers were taught how to combine as a unit to penetrate the opponents' defence using physical strength and intelligence in devising tactics to out-manoeuvre the opposition.

The game was taken up by Britons after the Roman garrisons were withdrawn. It retained the military objective but was contested between villages and towns. This led to the mob-football described earlier.

Around the 16th century the game became established in schools but, to maintain order and discipline, codes of conduct were drawn up to regulate play. A common feature of these early school games was emphasis on combined effort and team play with players moving as a unit behind the ball towards the defined target.

Any player caught in advance of the ball was considered to be out-of-play, off-the-side, offside. In military terms he was out of the battle, out of his unit, off-the-strength.

In the sporting context to be offside was unfair as indicated in the rules of school games in the last century:

No player is allowed to loiter between the ball and the adversaries' goal. (Cambridge Rules, 1856)
A player is "out-of-play" immediately he is in front of the ball and must return behind the ball as soon as possible. (Uppingham School, 1860)
A player is considered to be "sneaking" when only three or less opponents are before him and the opponents behind him. In such case he may not kick the ball. (Eton College, 1862)

The detail of early offside rules stresses the same point, that the player had no right to interfere with play or an opponent. This restriction has influenced tactics of defence in moving forward to leave an opponent in limbo, the so called "offside trap", accepted as a legitimate game strategy. Attackers must be alert to avoid being caught "behind enemy lines".

To underline the point that offside is unfair play we know from our own experience as children that the player we despised the most was the one who placed himself close to goal waiting to score. The "goal-poacher", "goal-hanger", made little effort to help the other players, seeking the glory of scoring with the minimum of skill. At 6 or 7 years we did not understand the formal offside law but inner feelings told us that this was not playing the game as it should be played.

Other team sports, rugby, hockey, even water polo, include an offside rule on the same principle that attacking moves should develop as a combined team effort rather than rely on individual opportunism. The rule demands alertness and intelligence both on the part of attackers and defenders to constantly assess tactical movements and devise counter measures. It contributes much to the attractive fluidity and interest of the play.

Players who know the offside law can improve performance to the benefit of the team. As an example, in an important international match, a famous England player destroyed eight potential goal-scoring moves by being caught offside. One or two are excusable but not eight. The player did not understand the law or how to avoid offside situations. In another match, previously mentioned, English players were ruled offside on twenty of the twenty-two occasions recorded. The result was close, England won 1-0.

How does the offside law work?
Every offside situation involves just two basic elements:
   1. Fact: the actual *position* of a player at *the moment the ball is played* by a team-mate, and
   2. Opinion: whether he is *interfering* with play, or an opponent, or trying to gain an *unfair advantage.*

If a player is in advance of the ball, is not level with or does not have two or more opponents between himself and the goal line, he is in an OFFSIDE POSITION. This is a fact. To avoid being judged offside the player must either return behind the ball, before it is played in his direction by a team-mate, or keep well clear of play and opponents involved in the active play, because the referee has to form an opinion as to why he is in that position and his influence on the play.

If the England player had understood these simple elements he could have taken action to evade at least four offside decisions. One of these occasions could have enabled an attack to result in the winning goal.

Why should offside cause so much controversy? Basically, the problem is related to timing and difference of opinion.

Judgement of offside position starts at the moment the ball is played. The referee and linesman must freeze in their minds the actual positions of attacking and defending players. This is rarely taken into account by players and spectators because of the natural tendency to follow the movement of the ball. The referee does not always stop play immediately because if the ball is kicked a long distance forward he needs time to judge whether the player, in an offside position, is seeking to gain an advantage or will be close enough, when the ball arrives, to influence the next phase of play.

Each situation is seldom black or white. A player in an offside position near the left touch line will not be penalised if the ball is passed towards an on-side player near the right touch line. He is too far away to interfere with the play.

In a similar incident but where the first player is near the centre of the field - a grey area - the referee must assess the player's actions and intentions before making a decision. In the meantime players' positions can change during the time taken for the ball to arrive in the next area of play. A perfectly correct offside decision can appear unjust if the penalised player receives the ball in an on-side position. Conversely, a player may appear to be offside but is not penalised because he has moved forward, from an on-side position, after the ball was kicked by a team-mate.

To assist referees, in judging interference and intention to gain advantage, the International Board stated, in 1924:

If a player in an offside position advances towards an opponent or the ball and, in so doing, causes the play to be affected he should be penalised.

Judging offside situations requires intense concentration by referees and linesmen, particularly when players' positions change rapidly. Because split-second decisions must be formed on the factors described a match official may err occasionally but not as often as it may seem from the point of view of the player or spectator.

A player is not penalised for offside if he receives the ball direct from a goal kick, a corner kick or from a throw-in.

Summarising, the offside law is a basic element of a team game where an objective is to be achieved through the combined skills of a group of players. It contributes to the fluidity of play, and tests alertness, intelligence and tactical innovation.

Offside can be avoided if players remember three simple rules:

1. remain behind the ball, or,
2. keep at least two opponents between yourself and the goal line; or,
3. keep clear of the next phase of play if in an offside position.

Offside judgements start at the moment the ball is played. Match officials concentrate on this factor while others tend to follow the ball. Interfering or attempting to gain an advantage are matters of opinion based on the actions and intentions of players in an offside position.

The following diagrams show several examples of offside situations based on the positions of players (circled) when the ball is played.

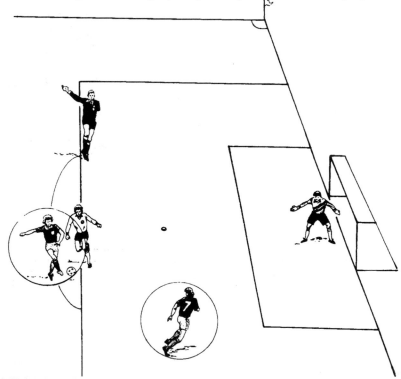

At the moment the ball is played number 7 is IN AN OFFSIDE POSITION (not having at least two opponents between himself and the goal line). He is clearly taking advantage (OPINION). Decision: OFFSIDE

At the moment the ball is played number 7 is NOT IN AN OFFSIDE POSITION (having at least two opponents between himself and the goal line). Decision: NOT OFFSIDE

Note: In each diagram the circles denote the positions of the players at the moment the ball is played.

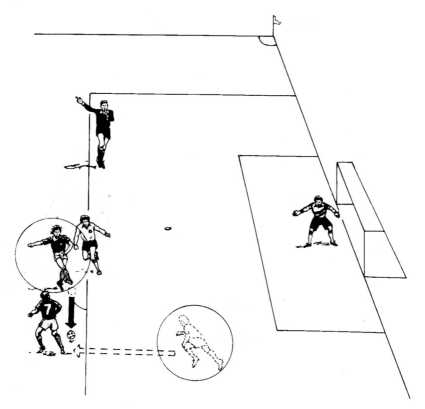

At the moment the ball is played number 7 is IN AN OFFSIDE POSITION. He cannot change this fact by running back to receive the ball in an on-side position. Decision: OFFSIDE

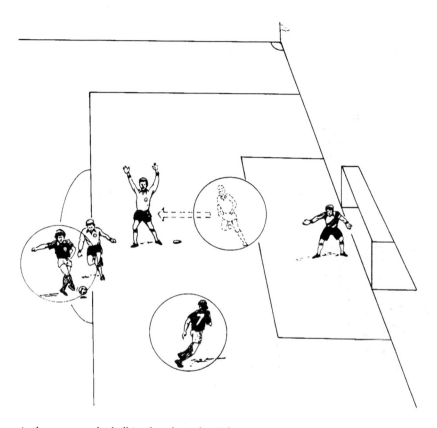

At the moment the ball is played number 7 has two opponents between himself and the goal line. He is, therefore, NOT IN AN OFFSIDE POSITION. The opponent cannot change this fact by running forward. Decision: NOT OFFSIDE

At the moment the ball is played number 11 is IN AN OFFSIDE POSITION (FACT) but is NOT INTERFERING WITH PLAY (OPINION). Decision: NOT OFFSIDE

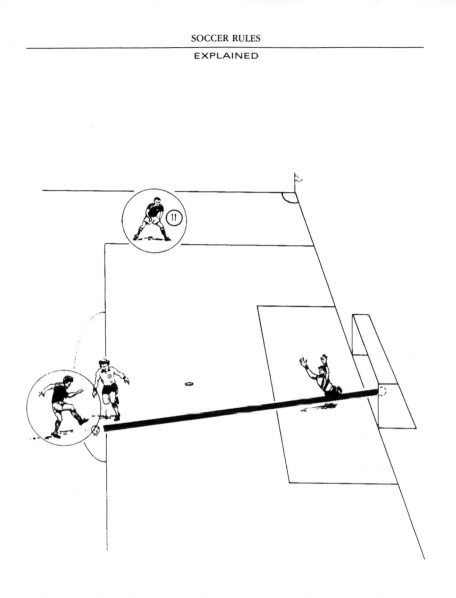

At the moment the ball is played number 11 is IN AN OFFSIDE POSITION but is NOT INTERFERING with play when the ball is kicked directly into the goal. Decision: A GOAL

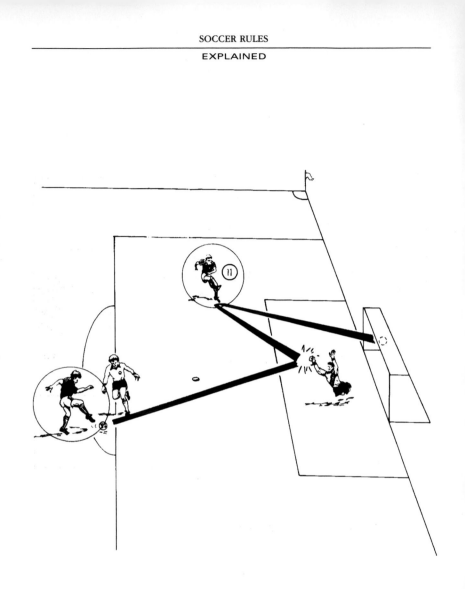

At the moment the ball is played number 11 is IN AN OFFSIDE POSITION. The ball is played by an opponent (goalkeeper) and he scores. The goal should be disallowed for OFFSIDE because number 11 clearly gained an advantage from an offside position.

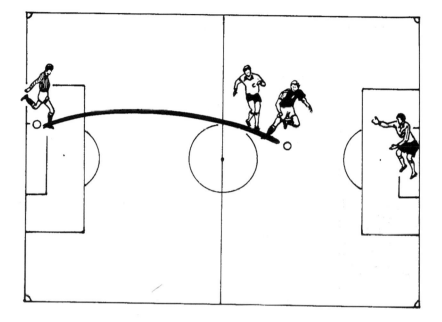

A player is NOT OFFSIDE if the ball is received direct from a goal kick

A player is NOT OFF-SIDE if the ball is received direct from a corner-kick

A player is NOT OFFSIDE if the ball is received direct from a throw-in

Law 11 - Offside

Offside Position

It is not an offence in itself to be in an offside position.

A player is in an offside position if:

● *he is nearer to his opponents' goal line than both the ball and the second last opponent*

A player is not in an offside position if:

● *he is in his own half of the field of play*

or

● *he is level with the second last opponent*

or

● *he is level with the last two opponents*

Offence

A player in an offside position is only penalised if, at the moment the ball touches or is played by one of his team, he is, in the opinion of the referee, involved in active play by:

● *interfering with play*
● *interfering with an opponent*
● *gaining an advantage by being in that position*

No Offence

There is no offside offence if a player receives the ball directly from:

● *a goal kick*

or

● *a throw-in*

or

● *a corner kick*

Infringements/Sanctions

For any offside offence, the referee awards an indirect free kick to the opposing team to be taken from the place where the infringement occurred.* (see Law 8)

9
Discipline

Physical and moral codes

Soccer was chosen by educationalists as a sport to strengthen bodies and to develop desirable qualities of character such as self-discipline, responsibility and a sense of justice.

Law 12 allows for the game to be played in a robust but fair manner demanding physical effort while providing limits which enables players to exercise skills which they and others can enjoy.

The desired code of discipline is clear from the description of actions considered as misconduct in the third part of the law.

Law 12 - Fouls and Misconduct

This law is the backbone of soccer. It provides the elements necessary to enable players to demonstrate their skills in a physical contact game within a code of conduct based on fair play to obtain the maximum of pleasure.

Fouls (unfair play) and misconduct, considered to be crimes against the intended method of play or the spirit of the game, are regulated by four punishments of varying degrees:

INDIRECT FREE KICK: for minor or technical offences
DIRECT FREE KICK: for more serious offences;
CAUTION: an official warning against repetition of unfair play;
DISMISSAL: exclusion from the match.

The law can be separated into three parts: penal offences, technical offences and misconduct.

Penal Offences

The first part of the law lists ten offences for which a direct free kick is awarded. They are usually referred to as penal offences because, if committed by a defending player within his own penalty area, the direct freekick becomes a penalty kick, a severe punishment which normally results in a goal. Law 14 describes the procedure for penalty kicks.

The first principle of equality of opportunity to demonstrate personal skills provides that, when the ball is in play any player has the right to challenge for its possession. Opposing players have the same right. Challenges often involve physical contact which is acceptable (fair) or unacceptable (unfair).

In judging what is fair and unfair the law requires the referee to penalise actions considered to be "careless, reckless or using excessive force". Dictionary definitions do not provide clear dividing lines between these three terms. In practice, they fuse into one simple category of "unfair" actions.

Until 1996 referees were instructed to read the "intention" of the player to differentiate between fair and unfair actions. Now, the decision depends on what each referee constitutes fair and unfair play. This has to be a variable factor according to individual appreciation of how the game should be played within the tradition and spirit behind the written law.

Nine of the ten penal offences specify unfair actions against opponents.

Most referees have played the game, many still do. Having been on the receiving end (or the instigator) of unfair kicking, tripping, jumping for the ball, charging, striking and pushing, they know instinctively when an action is "careless, reckless or involves excessive force". No time to refer to the dictionary, the action is either acceptable or unacceptable (fair or unfair) - play on or stop.

The offences of holding an opponent or spitting at an opponent are clearly unacceptable but the offence of "tackling to obtain possession which involves contact with an opponent before touching the ball" needs some explanation.

Tackling, in other forms of football, e.g. rugby, American, Australian Rules, involves using hands and arms to grapple an opponent. In soccer tackling is restricted to using feet and legs directed at the ball. When referees applied the previous yardstick of "intention" a player could not be penalised for "accidentally" making contact with the opponent when "intentionally" playing the ball. Aggressive defenders found this a useful loophole and were encouraged to destroy skilful players with increasing violence of physical contact.

The so-called "tackle from behind" grew from a subtle touch, to warn the player in possession that an opponent was close behind, to horrendous uncontrolled blocking with the whole body, tackling the player first in the guise of going for the ball.

For twenty years the IFAB appealed to players and referees to rid the game of this aspect of play to the point where the following directive became necessary in 1990:

A tackle from behind, which is violent with little or no attempt to play the ball, is prohibited and will be punished by a direct free kick and dismissal of the offender.

Penal offence: kicking an opponent.

Some progress is being made. Defenders are more cautious and the skills of exciting players are more evident. However, the problem has not gone away. Only strict observance of the directive by referees will liberate the full potential of talented soccer players. That is the dream of all fair-minded soccer lovers. If it ever becomes reality that will really be something to see!

The tenth offence, handling the ball, contravenes the basic method of play decided over 100 years ago. This was a fundamental change from earlier games where hands could be used to control the ball.

Tripping? Holding? or Fair? The referee must decide. Photo: Pro Sport.

Destroyer of much skill, the deliberate tackle from behind is prohibited. A penal offence which can be punished by dismissal.

Penal offence: jumping at an opponent.

Penal offence: charging which is careless, reckless or involves excessive force.

Who is holding? Who is pushing? Who should be punished? Photo: Presse Sports.

Penal offence: holding. No doubt about intention here.

Penal offence: handling the ball. A penalty kick here and dismissal if the referee considers that the opponents have been denied an obvious goal-scoring opportunity (Sending off offence 4).

This is SERIOUS FOUL PLAY intended to destroy an obvious goal-scoring opportunity.
The offender must be dismissed and a penalty kick awarded if the offence occurred
inside the penalty area (Sending off offence 5).

The tradition was not easy to break. It is said that, to discourage converts to the game from handling, a group of enterprising ex-Harrow-School graduates provided players with white silk gloves and valuable silver coins to be held in the hands during play. It is not recorded whether this practice was effective but there is no doubt that soccer became very popular in the Yorkshire area where it was introduced. Handling the ball is judged on intention. Ball to hand situations, e.g. when protecting the body from impact, are acceptable. Hand to ball, to gain an advantage, is not.

In recent years a trend towards deliberate handling, to deny opponents a clear goal-scoring opportunity, caused the International Board to decide, in 1991, that this offence should be classed as serious foul play requiring the referee to dismiss the offender (Sending off offence 4).

This decision was a logical extension of another decision, announced in 1990, that a player who intentionally impedes an opponent and denies his team an obvious goal-scoring opportunity must be dismissed (Sending off offence 5).

Impeding or obstruction. When not playing the ball, number 3 intentionally runs between the opponent and the ball, indirect free kick

Technical Offences

The second part of Law 12 lists eight offences punishable by an indirect free kick. Three concern mainly outfield players, the rest are specific to goalkeepers. The first, dangerous play, covers any action which the referee considers dangerous to an opponent beyond the reasonable norm of danger to be expected in a physical contact sport. Examples include kicking at the ball, or using an overhead or "bicycle" kicking action, when the ball is close to the head or body of an opponent.

Before the 1997 version of the laws was approved Law 12 included a specific offence of "charging fairly, i.e. with the shoulder, when the ball is not within playing distance of the players concerned and they are definitely not trying to play it".

Charging an opponent has always been one of the acceptable physical challenges for possession of the ball. The object is to put the opponent off balance with shoulder to shoulder contact without being "careless, reckless or using excessive force".

Fair charging is only an offence when the ball is not within playing distance. Playing distance means that the player can play the ball if he so wishes.

It is an offence to "impede the progress of an opponent" by running

Technical offence: Dangerous play.

between the opponent and the ball, or interposing the body so as to form an obstacle thus denying an opponent a fair challenge for the ball.

It applies also to impeding a goalkeeper from putting the ball into play.

For many decades legitimate goals could be scored by charging the goalkeeper into his own goal while he was holding the ball. In British soccer this was fair compensation against the goalkeeper's privilege of handling the ball but other soccer areas frowned on such direct attacks on the guardian of the goal and the practice gradually disappeared from the game.

It is now rare to see a fair charge on a goalkeeper. Protection has evolved to the point where goalkeepers are allowed almost uncontested possession of the ball inside the whole of the penalty area. This unintended freedom has led to tactics which exaggerated the role and influence of the goalkeeper to the detriment of attacking play.

Effectively the ball is unplayable once in the goalkeeper's hands. Law 12 lists five offences to discourage the goalkeeper from unreasonable ball possession.

To discourage the negative tactic of deliberately kicking the ball back into the goalkeeper's hands, by a defender under challenge, the International Board decided, in 1992, to remove the handling privilege in this situation and to punish any breach by the award of an indirect free kick against the goalkeeper. This was extended, in 1997, to include receiving the ball into the goalkeeper's hands from a throw-in taken by a team-mate.

The message to goalkeepers is clear - you have protection to defend your goal but no right to excessive possession of the ball.

Misconduct

The final part of Law 12 specifies sanctions for offences against the code of behaviour required to maintain the game as a disciplined and honourable sport. While such a code is not stated it can be deduced by inversion of the listed offences thus:

● respect the ethics of sportsmanship and fair play;

Showing dissent, by word or action from any decision given by the referee. The player is cautioned and dismissed on further misconduct.

- know the laws of the game to avoid offences;
- accept decisions of match officials without question;
- understand that the referee must know, at all times, precisely who may be on the field to participate in the play;
- control the force and timing of challenges for the ball;
- discipline your language.

For 100 years the law included the cautionable offence of "ungentlemanly conduct", a reminder that the original laws were prescribed for "gentleman" players. Now, it is the more appropriate "unsporting behaviour" which covers all classes of players.

The referee indicates a "caution" by displaying a yellow card and a "dismissal" with a red card. Both punishments are reported to a competent authority (a league or organising body) for further action which may take the form of a fine or suspension from playing for a number of matches or a determined period.

An offence, which is not mentioned in the laws but which is important in relation to the desired code of conduct, is that of "bringing the game into disrepute". It covers any act which degrades the honour and good reputation of soccer. Such acts are serious breaches of sporting etiquette. Examples would include deliberate attempts to affect the results of matches by bribery, cheating or corruption. A specific case has been described in comments relative to Law 7 (page 101). Administrators with responsibilities for protecting the good name of soccer, in addition to players, are subject to disciplinary measures if found guilty of this offence.

Summarising, this law incorporates the physical, ethical and moral codes necessary for players to take part in a healthy sport, to exercise personal skills within a team game for their own pleasure and that of others who watch them play.

Law 12 - Fouls and Misconduct

Fouls and misconduct are penalised as follows:

Direct Free Kick

A direct free kick is awarded to the opposing team if a player commits any of the following six offences in a manner considered by the referee to be careless, reckless or using excessive force:

- *kicks or attempts to kick an opponent*
- *trips or attempts to trip an opponent*
- *jumps at an opponent*
- *charges an opponent*
- *strikes or attempts to strike an opponent*
- *pushes an opponent*

A direct free kick is also awarded to the opposing team if a player commits any of the following four offences:

- *tackles an opponent to gain possession of the ball making contact with the opponent before touching the ball*
- *holds an opponent*
- *spits at an opponent*
- *handles the ball deliberately (except for the goalkeeper within his own penalty area)*

A direct free kick is taken from where the offence occurred.* (see Law 8).

Penalty Kick

A penalty kick is awarded if any of the above ten offences is committed by a player inside his own penalty area, irrespective of the position of the ball, provided it is in play.

Indirect Free Kick

An indirect free kick is awarded to the opposing team if a player, in the opinion of the referee, commits any of the following three offences:

● *plays in a dangerous manner*
● *impedes the progress of an opponent*
● *prevents the goalkeeper from releasing the ball from his hands*

An indirect free kick is also awarded to the opposing team if a goalkeeper, inside his own penalty area, commits any of the following five offences:

● *takes more than four steps while controlling the ball with his hands, before releasing it from his possession*
● *touches the ball again with his hands after it has been released from his possession and has not touched any other player*
● *touches the ball with his hands after it has been deliberately kicked to him by a team-mate*
● *touches the ball with his hands after he has received it directly from a throw-in taken by a team-mate*
● *wastes time*

The indirect free kick is taken from where the offence occurred.* (see Law 8)

Disciplinary Sanctions

Cautionable Offences

A player is cautioned and shown the yellow card if he commits any of the following seven offences:

1. is guilty of unsporting behaviour
2. shows dissent by word or action
3. persistently infringes the Laws of the Game
4. delays the restart of play
5. fails to respect the required distance when play is restarted with a corner kick or free kick
6. enters or re-enters the field of play without the referee's permission
7. deliberately leaves the field of play without the referee's permission

Sending-Off Offences

A player is sent off and shown the red card if he commits any of the following seven offences:

1. is guilty of serious foul play

2. is guilty of violent conduct

3. spits at an opponent or any other person

4. denies an opponent a goal or an obvious goal-scoring opportunity by deliberately handling the ball (this does not apply to a goalkeeper within his own penalty area)

5. denies an obvious goal-scoring opportunity to an opponent moving towards the player's goal by an offence punishable by a free kick or a penalty kick

6. uses offensive, insulting or abusive language

7. receives a second caution in the same match

Decisions of the International F.A. Board

● Decision 1

A penalty kick is awarded if, while the ball is in play, the goalkeeper, inside his own penalty area, strikes or attempts to strike an opponent by throwing the ball at him.

● Decision 2

A player who commits a cautionable or sending-off offence, either on or off the field of play, whether directed towards an opponent, a team-mate, the referee, an assistant referee or any other person, is disciplined according to the nature of the offence committed.

● Decision 3

The goalkeeper is considered to be in control of the ball by touching it with any part of his hand or arms. Possession of the ball includes the goalkeeper deliberately parrying the ball, but does not include the circumstances where, in the opinion of the referee, the ball rebounds accidentally from the goalkeeper, for example after he has made a save.

● Decision 4

Subject to the terms of Law 12, a player may pass the ball to his own goalkeeper using his head or chest or knee, etc. If, however, in the opinion of the referee, a player uses a deliberate trick while the ball is in play in order to circumvent the Law, the player is guilty of unsporting behaviour. He is cautioned, shown the yellow card and an indirect free kick is awarded to the opposing team from the place where the infringement occurred.*(see Law 8). A player using a deliberate trick to circumvent the Law while he is taking a free kick is cautioned for unsporting behaviour and shown the yellow card. The free kick is retaken. In such circumstances, it is irrelevant whether the goalkeeper subsequently touches the ball with his hands or not. The offence is committed by the player in attempting to circumvent both the letter and the spirit of Law 12.

10
Restarts

Simple procedures for restarting play

This final group of laws, 13, 14, 15, 16 and 17, deals with the procedure of restarting the game after it has been stopped by the referee for an infringement or after the ball has crossed a boundary line.

An essential principle is to get the ball back into play in a simple fashion and with the minimum of delay. A common feature of these five laws, plus Law 8, is that the player putting the ball into play is not allowed to touch it again until it has been touched by another player. He must release the ball and not run with it.

Law 13 - Free Kicks

Hardly any soccer game is completed without free kicks being awarded for offences of the nature described in the previous law. Numbers can vary according to the sporting attitude and conduct of the players.

The 52 matches of the USA '94 World Cup averaged 30 free kicks with a low of 16 (Brazil v. Sweden) and a high of 42 (Bulgaria v. Greece)

This law describes the conditions for the correct procedure for putting the ball into play after a free kick is awarded.

There are two categories of free kick:

a. DIRECT: a goal can be scored if the ball goes directly into the opponents' goal; and,

b. INDIRECT: a goal cannot be scored unless the ball is touched by a player other than the kicker.

For a direct free kick, awarded for any of the penal offences listed in Law 12, the referee points the direction in which the kick shall be taken or to the penalty spot if a defender has committed the offence inside his own penalty area.

To indicate that a free kick is indirect the referee raises one arm above his head.

Definition: A FREE KICK is the privilege of Kicking the Ball, without obstruction in such a manner as the Kicker may think fit. (Original definition, 1863)

As a free kick is intended to compensate the non-offending team for an offence committed by their opponents the definition provides for a FREE-FROM-OBSTRUCTION KICK.

A frequent tactic in soccer is the formation of a "wall" of defenders between the ball and the goal. It is not illegal but any action intended to delay the kick or encroaching into the "free from obstruction" area, i.e. 10 yards radius from the ball, before the ball is kicked into play, is considered as a serious breach of fair play.

The problem is not new for the International Board issued a firm instruction to referees, in 1910. It reads:

The defensive "wall". Photo: Pro Sport.

Direct Free-kick Signal

Indirect Free-kick Signal

Free kicks, direct and indirect.

ree - kick — Goal

ect — Goal

Players who do not retire to the proper distance when a free kick is taken MUST be CAUTIONED and on any repetition ORDERED OFF.

As already explained in Law 5 the referee may decide to allow a freekick to be taken before the 10-yards limit is observed to deny the opposing team any advantage in delay. It is a practice to be encouraged in the interests of fair play.

A player cannot score a goal against his own side from a free kick because the kick has been awarded to punish the offending team. Play is restarted with a corner kick.

Law 13 - Free Kicks

Types of Free Kicks

Free kicks are either direct or indirect.

For both direct and indirect free kicks, the ball must be stationary when the kick is taken and the kicker does not touch the ball a second time until it has touched another player.

The Direct Free Kick

● *if a direct free kick is kicked directly into the opponents' goal, a goal is awarded*

● *if a direct free kick is kicked directly into the teams' own goal, a corner kick is awarded to the opposing team*

The Indirect Free Kick

Signal

The referee indicates an indirect free kick by raising his arm above his head. He maintains his arm in that position until the kick has been taken and the ball has touched another player or goes out of play.

Ball Enters the Goal

A goal can be scored only if the ball subsequently touches another player before it enters the goal.

● *if an indirect free kick is kicked directly into the opponents' goal, a goal kick is awarded*

● *if an indirect free kick is kicked directly into the teams' own goal, a corner kick is awarded to the opposing team*

Position of Free Kick

Free Kick Inside the Penalty Area

Direct or indirect free kick to the defending team:

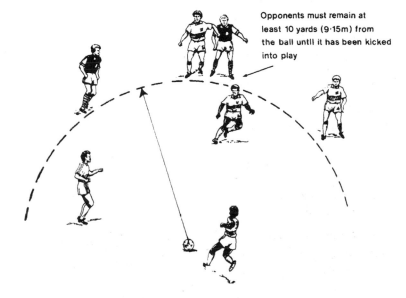

Opponents must remain at least 10 yards (9·15m) from the ball until it has been kicked into play

Free kicks must not be obstructed by opponents. They must remain at least 10 yards (9.15 metres) from the ball until it has been kicked into play.

- all opponents are at least 9.15 m (10 yds) from the ball
- all opponents remain outside the penalty area until the ball is in play
- the ball is in play when it is kicked directly beyond the penalty area
- a free kick awarded in the goal area is taken from any point inside that area

Indirect free kick to the attacking team:

- all opponents are at least 9.15 m (10 yds) from the ball until it is in play, unless they are on their own goal line between the goal-posts
- the ball is in play when it is kicked and moves
- an indirect free kick awarded inside the goal area is taken from that part of the goal area line which runs parallel to the goal line, at the point nearest to where the infringement occurred

Free Kick Outside the Penalty Area

- all opponents are at least 9.15 m (10 yds) from the ball until it is in play
- the ball is in play when it is kicked and moves

- the free kick is taken from the place where the infringement occurred

Infringements/Sanctions

If, when a free kick is taken, an opponent is closer to the ball than the required distance:

- the kick is retaken

If, when a free kick is taken by the defending team from inside its own penalty area, the ball is not kicked directly into play:

- the kick is retaken

Free kick taken by a player other than the goalkeeper

If, after the ball is in play, the kicker touches the ball a second time (except with his hands) before it has touched another player:

- an indirect free kick is awarded to the opposing team, the kick to be taken from the place where the infringement occurred *

If, after the ball is in play, the kicker deliberately handles the ball before it has touched another player:

- a direct free kick is awarded to the opposing team, the kick to be taken from the place where the infringement occurred *

● *a penalty kick is awarded if the infringement occurred inside the kicker's penalty area*

Free kick taken by the goalkeeper
If, after the ball is in play, the goalkeeper touches the ball a second time (except with his hands), before it has touched another player:

● *an indirect free kick is awarded to the opposing team, the kick to be taken from the place where the infringement occurred**

If, after the ball is in play, the goalkeeper deliberately handles the ball before it has touched another player:

● *a direct free kick is awarded to the opposing team if the infringement occurred outside the goalkeeper's penalty area, the kick to be taken from the place where the infringement occurred**

● *an indirect free kick is awarded to the opposing team if the infringement occurred inside the goalkeeper's penalty area, the kick to be taken from the place where the infringement occurred. **

* See Special Circumstances Law 8

Law 14 - The Penalty Kick

Just one penalty kick can decide the whole of a soccer match, even the winner of a World Cup Final, as happened in the eighty-fifth minute of the 1990 final when Brehme converted from the penalty mark for Germany against Argentina.

First introduced in 1891 the penalty kick was intended to counter abuses by a growing number of professional players who employed any illegal means to prevent goals being scored. Deliberate handling was one of the main violations and the incident which finally convinced opponents to a penalty kick occurred in an FA Quarter Final match between Stoke City and Notts County early in 1891. Notts were leading 1-0 until the last minute when a defender punched the ball away as it was about to enter the goal. At that time the punishment was a free kick which was awarded to Stoke near to the goal line. The kick was blocked and Notts County won the match, subsequently to appear in the final where they lost to Blackburn Rovers.

The penalty kick which won the 1990 World Cup for Germany against Argentina. Brehme puts the ball out of reach of goalkeeper Goyochea. Photo: Pro Sport.

Penalty kick: introduced in 1891 to counter a "professional foul".

Penalty kick: not intended for "gentleman" players!

Amateur players ignored the new law for some years considering that it applied only to paid players. They took the view that a penalty kick awarded against their team was a slur on their moral behaviour to the point where the captain would instruct his goalkeeper to stand by a corner post to leave the goal unprotected when the kick was taken.

While sympathising with this ethical point of view the lawmakers insisted that the law must be enforced. Thus, it was amended to require the goalkeeper to stand on his goal line "between the goalposts".

The object of the law is to provide a punishment to fit the crime. One of the direct free kick offences, listed in Law 12, has been committed and the team offended against should have a reasonable chance to redress the situation. However, a penalty kick does not guarantee a goal - about 90% are converted - it becomes a test of skill between the kicker and the goalkeeper with the odds on the former. The interest is in how the two principal actors combat each other's skills.

The requirement that the goalkeeper must, "stand on his own goal line until the ball is kicked", was introduced in 1905 to cancel the goalkeeper's liberty to advance up to six yards towards the ball which had resulted in too many unsuccessful penalties. In 1929 a further restriction, to stop goalkeepers from moving laterally, was imposed requiring that the goalkeeper must, "stand (without moving his feet) on his own goal line".

This last restriction was gradually ignored by goalkeepers and referees to the 1990's situation where goalkeeper movement, along and from the goal line, occurred in nearly 70% of penalty kicks.

The 1997 law revision seems to have accepted defeat in controlling movement along the goal line. The goalkeeper now needs only to "remain on his goal-line . . . until the ball has been kicked."

Goalkeepers have grabbed this freedom with both feet(!) Abuses are already evident with increased movement from the goal line. The split-second advantage pays off enough times to be worth trying for the law only requires a retake of the penalty kick if the referee decides to sanction.

The law is precise in the organisation of a penalty kick. Only the kicker and the goalkeeper are allowed inside the penalty area, all other players must remain at least 10 yards from the ball, outside the penalty area, and behind the penalty mark.

As in other Laws the kicker must not play the ball a second time until it has been touched by another player.

The reason for extending time, to allow a penalty kick to be completed, has been explained in comments on Law 7 (Duration of the Match).

Penalty tie-breakers, or "shoot-outs", have become a feature of soccer in knock-out competitions where a match is drawn but a "winner" has to be determined to proceed to the next stage or receive a trophy in a final game. This procedure replaced the previous unsatisfactory ceremony, of tossing a coin or drawing lots, in 1970. "Shoot-outs" are not part of the match and do not nullify the criteria for deciding the result as laid down in Law 10 (The Method of Scoring).

The special conditions to be met, at a penalty kick ceremony, are that each team is allowed five kicks. The team "scoring" the most goals is declared the winner. If there is no result after the initial series of kicks the teams take alternative kicks until there is one goal difference after an equal number of attempts. The full procedure is detailed on page 179.

The 1994 World Cup Final was decided by this system. Brazil were declared winners by achieving three successful kicks to Italy's two.

Law 14 - The Penalty Kick

A penalty kick is awarded against a team which commits one of the ten offences for which a direct free kick is awarded, inside its own penalty area and while the ball is in play.

A goal may be scored directly from a penalty kick.

Additional time is allowed for a penalty kick to be taken at the end of each half or at the end of periods of extra time.

Position of the Ball and the Players
The ball:

● *is placed on the penalty mark*

The player taking the penalty kick:

● *is properly identified*

The defending goalkeeper:

● *remains on his goal line, facing the kicker between the goalposts until the ball has been kicked*

The players other than the kicker are located:

● *inside the field of play*
● *outside the penalty area*
● *behind the penalty mark*
● *at least 9.15 m (10 yds) from the penalty mark*

The Referee

● *does not signal for a penalty kick to be taken until the players have taken up position in accordance with the Law*
● *decides when a penalty kick has been completed*

Procedure

● *the player taking the penalty kicks the ball forward*
● *he does not play the ball a second time until it has touched another player*
● *the ball is in play when it is kicked and moves forward*

When a penalty kick is taken during the normal course of play, or time has been extended at half-time or full time to allow a penalty kick to be taken or retaken, a goal is awarded if, before passing between the goalposts and under the crossbar:

● *the ball touches either or both of the goalposts and/or the cross-bar and/or the goalkeeper*

Infringements/Sanctions

If the referee gives the signal for a penalty kick to be taken and, before the ball is in play, one of the following situations occurs:

The player taking the penalty kick infringes the Laws of the Game:

● *the referee allows the kick to proceed*
● *if the ball enters the goal, the kick is retaken*
● *if the ball does not enter the goal, the kick is not retaken*

The goalkeeper infringes the Laws of the Game:

● *the referee allows the kick to proceed*
● *if the ball enters the goal, a goal is awarded*
● *if the ball does not enter the goal, the kick is retaken*

All players, except the kicker, must remain outside the penalty area and behind the penalty mark until the ball has been kicked into play. The goalkeeper must remain on his goal-line, between the posts.

A team-mate of the player taking the kick enters the penalty area or moves in front of or within 9.15 (10 yds) of the penalty mark:

● *the referee allows the kick to proceed*
● *if the ball enters the goal, the kick is retaken*
● *if the ball does not enter the goal, the kick is not retaken*

A team-mate of the goalkeeper enters the penalty area or moves in front of or within 9.15 m (10 yds) of the penalty mark:

● *the referee allows the kick to proceed*
● *if the ball enters the goal a goal is awarded*
● *if the ball does not enter the goal the kick is retaken*

A player of both the defending team and the attacking team infringe the Laws of the Game:

● *the kick is retaken*

If after the penalty kick has been taken:

The kicker touches the ball a second time (except with his hands) before it has touched another player:

● *an in direct free kick is awarded to the opposing team the kick to be taken from the place where the infringement occurred* (see Law 8)*

The kicker deliberately handles the ball before it has touched another player:

● *a direct free kick is awarded to the opposing team, the kick to be taken from the place where the infringement occurred * (see Law 8)*

The ball is touched by an outside agent as it moves forward:

● *the kick is retaken*

The ball rebounds into the field of play from the goalkeeper, the crossbar or the goalposts, and is then touched by an outside agent:

● *the referee stops play*
● *play is restarted with a dropped ball at the place where it touched the outside agent* (see Law 8)*

Law 15 - The Throw-in

The number of throw-ins can vary from twenty, in a match played on a large field by skilled players, to nearly a hundred in a low-skill game played on a small field with difficult wind conditions.

Although the object is to get the ball back into play quickly and fairly a throw-in can have important tactical advantages. Some players develop skill in throwing the ball long distances. The two-handed throwing method was adopted in 1882 from a proposal of the Scottish FA. It replaced the one-handed method which was seen to be unfair when William Gunn, an English international, often propelled the ball the whole length of the field.

The law is precise in describing the correct method of throwing in. Any improper throw is punished by awarding a throw-in to the opposing team.

Remembering that offside does not apply, a throw-in, taken in the opponents' half, can lead to a goal if the ball is thrown into the goal, although it must first be touched by another player. Should the ball pass directly into the goal the play is restarted with a goal kick.

Sometimes a player will deliberately kick the ball over a touch line in order to stop the game when another player appears to be seriously

The one-handed throw-in gave an unfair advantage.

Correct throw-in: 1 behind head, 2 over, 3 release. A continuous movement.

Incorrect: a push-throw.

Incorrect throw-in: both feet must remain on the ground, on or outside the touch line.

hurt. An interesting situation for the player is taking over the role of the referee whose duty it is to stop play for serious injury. The action is a considerate gesture of fair play which is invariably acknowledged in a practical manner by the team awarded the throw returning the ball immediately to their opponents.

Law 15 - The Throw-in

A throw-in is a method of restarting play.

A goal cannot be scored directly from a throw-in.

A throw-in is awarded:

- *when the whole of the ball passes over the touch line, either on the ground or in the air*
- *from the point where it crossed the touch line*
- *to the opponents of the player who last touched the ball*

Procedure

At the moment of delivering the ball, the thrower:

- *faces the field of play*
- *has part of each foot either on the touch line or on the ground outside the touch line*
- *uses both hands*
- *delivers the ball from behind and over his head*

The thrower may not touch the ball again until it has touched another player.

The ball is in play immediately it enters the field of play.

Infringements/Sanctions

Throw-in taken by a player other than the goalkeeper

If, after the ball is in play, the thrower touches the ball a second time (except with his hands) before it has touched another player:

- *an indirect free kick is awarded to the opposing team, the kick to be taken from the place where the infringement occurred* *

If, after the ball is in play, the thrower deliberately handles the ball before it has touched another player:

- *a direct free kick is awarded to the opposing team, the kick to be taken from the place where the infringement occurred* *

● *a penalty kick is awarded if the infringement occurred inside the thrower's penalty area*

Throw-in taken by the goalkeeper
If, after the ball is in play, the goalkeeper touches the ball a second time (except with his hands), before it has touched another player:

● *an indirect free kick is awarded to the opposing team, the kick to be taken from the place where the infringement occurred ***

If, after the ball is in play, the goalkeeper deliberately handles the ball before it has touched another player:

● *a direct free kick is awarded to the opposing team if the infringement occurred outside the goal-keeper's penalty area, the kick to he taken from the place where the infringement occurred ***

● *an indirect free kick is awarded to the opposing team if the infringement occurred inside the goalkeeper's penalty area, the kick to he taken from the place where the infringement occurred***

If an opponent unfairly distracts or impedes the thrower:

● *he is cautioned for unsporting behaviour and shown the yellow card*

For any other infringement of this Law:

● *the throw-in is taken by a player of the opposing team*

* See Special Circumstances Law 8

Law 16 - The Goal Kick

Depending on conditions the number of goal kicks in a soccer match can vary between ten and thirty. The average for the 1994 World Cup matches was twenty.

Effectively, the attacking team has failed to score when one of its players puts the ball over the opponent's goal line outside the goal. Possession of the ball is lost to the defending team and it is put back into play by a kick from the goal area. Although this task is often delegated to the goalkeeper it may be taken by any defender.

Goal kicks are usually either long or short. Long kicks can be effective, particularly with a following wind, in putting the ball into the opponents' half to forwards who cannot be offside from a goal kick. A disadvantage is that there is a fifty-fifty chance of the ball going to an opponent.

Short kicks, to a defender standing outside the penalty area, are usually intended to retain possession to develop an attack.

The ball is not in play until it has passed outside the penalty area.

Law 16 - The Goal Kick

A goal kick is a method of restarting play.

A goal may be scored directly from a goal kick, but only against the opposing team.

A goal kick is awarded when:

- *the whole of the ball, having last touched a player of the attacking team, passes over the goal line, either on the ground or in the air, and a goal is not scored in accordance with Law 10*

Procedure

- *the ball is kicked from any point within the goal area by a player of the defending team*
- *opponents remain outside the penalty area until the ball is in play*
- *the kicker does not play the ball a second time until it has touched another player*
- *the ball is in play when it is kicked directly beyond the penalty area*

Infringements/Sanctions
If the ball is not kicked directly into play beyond the penalty area:

● *the kick is retaken*

Goal kick taken by a player other than the goalkeeper
If, after the ball is in play, the kicker touches the ball a second time (except with his hands) before it has touched another player:

● *an indirect free kick is awarded to the opposing team, the kick to be taken from the place where the infringement occurred* *

If, after the ball is in play, the kicker deliberately handles the ball before it has touched another player:

● *a direct free kick is awarded to the opposing team, the kick to be taken from the place where the infringement occurred* *

● *a penalty kick is awarded if the infringement occurred inside the kicker's penalty area*

Goal kick taken by the goalkeeper
If, after the ball is in play, the goalkeeper touches the ball a second time (except with his hands) before it has touched another player:

● *an indirect free kick is awarded to the opposing team, the kick to be taken from the place where the infringement occurred* *

If, after the ball is in play, the goalkeeper deliberately handles the ball before it has touched another player:

● *a direct free kick is awarded to the opposing team if the infringement occurred outside the goalkeeper's penalty area, the kick to be taken from the place where the infringement occurred* *

● *an indirect free kick is awarded to the opposing team if the infringement occurred inside the goalkeeper's penalty area, the kick to be taken from the place where the infringement occurred* *

For any other infringement of this Law:

● *the kick is retaken*

* See Special Circumstances Law 8

Position of players at a goal kick: all players must remain outside the penalty area until the ball leaves the area. Defenders may be in the area.

Law 17 - The Corner Kick

Although few in number, varying between four and fifteen (1994 World Cup average: ten), corner kicks can be exciting because many players are usually positioned in the penalty area. It is a fact that a goal often results from a corner kick.

A corner kick is a form of compensation for the attacking team when an opponent puts the ball, intentionally or accidentally, over his own goal line outside of the goal. The kick is taken from the corner nearest to the point where the ball crossed the goal line. The corner quadrant limits the distance from the corner post and provides enough space for the ball to be kicked without danger of injury from the post (which must not be removed).

Corner kicks are opportunities for tactical innovation by attackers and defenders. Most corners are either long kicks into the goal area or short passes to an attacker to tempt defenders away from goal or to mount an attack from an unexpected angle. With good skill the ball can be swerved into the goal directly for a valid goal or swerved away from the goal to avoid the hands of the goalkeeper and find a well positioned team-mate.

Offside does not apply at corner kicks at the moment the ball is kicked, which allows attackers to position themselves on or close to the goal line.

If the ball rebounds to the kicker from a goalpost, or the referee, it must not be played again by him until touched by another player. This point was overlooked by the referee when Tottenham played Huddersfield in an important League match in 1952. From a corner kick the ball struck the referee, rebounded to the kicker who then passed it to team-mate to score. The referee, probably dazed by the impact of the ball, awarded a goal. Tottenham won the match 1-0 and Huddersfield were relegated to the Second Division despite filing a formal protest to the Football League and requesting that the match be replayed.

A classic case of the referee being right even when proved wrong. Upholding this principle was considered more important than the interests of one club. One year after this incident Huddersfield won back promotion to the First Division.

Every corner kick has potential for excitement and a goal

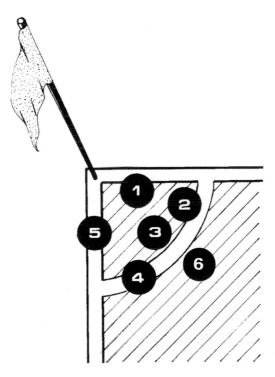

Placing the ball at a corner kick: correct - 1 to 5; incorrect - 6.

Corner kick: ball played a second time by the kicker, an error with serious consequences for Huddersfield Town

Law 17 - The Corner Kick

A corner kick is a method of restarting play.

A goal may be scored directly from a corner kick, but only against the opposing team.

A corner kick is awarded when:

● *the whole of the ball, having last touched a player of the defending team, passes over the goal line, either on the ground or in the air, and a goal is not scored in accordance with Law 10*

Procedure

● *the ball is placed inside the corner arc at the nearest corner flagpost*
● *the corner flagpost is not moved*
● *opponents remain at least 9.15 m (10 yds) from the ball until it is in play*
● *the ball is kicked by a player of the attacking team*
● *the ball is in play when it is kicked and moves*
● *the kicker does not play the ball a second time until it has touched another player*

Infringements/Sanctions

Corner kick taken by a player other than the goalkeeper

If, after the ball is in play, the kicker touches the ball a second time (except with his hands) before it has touched another player:

● *an indirect free kick is awarded to the opposing team, the kick to be taken from the place where the infringement occurred **

If, after the ball is in play, the kicker deliberately handles the ball before it has touched another player:

● *a direct free kick is awarded to the opposing team, the kick to be taken from the place where the infringement occurred **
● *a penalty kick is awarded if the infringement occurred inside the kicker's penalty area*

Corner kick taken by the goalkeeper

If, after the ball is in play, the goalkeeper touches the ball a second time (except with his hands) before it has touched another player:

175

● *an indirect free kick is awarded to the opposing team, the kick to be taken from the place where the infringement occurred* *

If, after the ball is in play, the goalkeeper deliberately handles the ball before it has touched another player:

● *a direct free kick is awarded to the opposing team if the infringement occurred outside the goalkeeper's penalty area, the kick to be taken from the place where the infringement occurred* *

● *an indirect free kick is awarded to the opposing team if the infringement occurred inside the goalkeeper's penalty area, the kick to be taken from the place where the infringement occurred* *

For any other infringement:

● *the kick is retaken*

* See Special Circumstances Law 8

Law 18 - Common Sense

Definition: "Common sense: sound practical judgement."

"Law 18" is an unwritten law invented by referees to be applied in situations where the formal laws do not provide a clear answer to a specific problem. The referee is on his own to weigh up the unforeseen situation and apply sound practical judgement based on his interpretation of fair play and justice.

A simple example would be where a corner post is broken during play and a replacement is not available. The referee would not abandon the match, because Law 1 insists on corner posts, but would find some way of marking the corner with a visible object after informing the captains of the problem.

The the prime object would be to conclude the match with the co-operation of the players.

The Technical Area

The technical area described in Law 3, International F.A. Board Decision 2, relates particularly to matches played in stadia with a designated seated area for technical staff and substitutes.

Technical areas may vary between stadia, for example in size or location, and the following notes are issued for general guidance.

● *The technical area extends 1 m (1 yd) on either side of the designated seated area and extends forward up to a distance of 1 m (1 yd) from the touch line.*

● *It is recommended that markings are used to define this area.*

● *The number of persons permitted to occupy the technical area is defined by the competition rules.*

● *The occupants of the technical area are identified before the beginning of the match in accordance with the competition rules.*

● *Only one person at a time is authorised to convey tactical instructions and he must return to his position immediately after giving these instructions.*

● *The coach and other officials must remain within the confines of the technical area except in special circumstances, for example, a physiotherapist or doctor entering the field of play, with the referee's permission, to assess an injured player.*

● *The coach and other occupants of the technical area must behave in a responsible manner*

The Fourth Official

● *The fourth official may be appointed under the competition rules and officiates if any of the three match officials is unable to continue.*

● *Prior to the start of the competition, the organiser states clearly whether, if the referee is unable to continue, the fourth official takes over as the match referee or whether the senior assistant referee takes over as referee with the fourth official becoming an assistant referee.*

● *The fourth official assists with any administrative duties before, during and after the match, as required by the referee.*

● *He is responsible for assisting with substitution procedures during the match.*

● *He supervises the replacement footballs, where required. If the match ball has to be replaced during a match, he provides another ball, on the instruction of the referee, thus keeping the delay to a minimum.*

● *He has the authority to check the equipment of substitutes before they enter the field of play. If their equipment does not comply with the Laws of the Game, he informs the assistant referee, who then informs the referee.*

● *The fourth official assists the referee at all times.*

● *After the match, the fourth official must submit a report to the appropriate authorities on any misconduct or other incident which has occurred out of the view of the referee and the assistant referees. The fourth official must advise the referee and his assistants of any report being made.*

Kicks from the Penalty Mark

Taking kicks from the penalty mark is a method of determining the winning team where competition rules require there to be a winning team after a match has been drawn

Procedure

- *The referee chooses the goal at which the kicks will be taken*
- *The referee tosses a coin and the team whose captain wins the toss takes the first kick*
- *The referee keeps a record of the kicks being taken*
- *Subject to the conditions explained below, both teams take five kicks*
- *The kicks are taken alternately by the teams*
- *If, before both teams have taken five kicks, one has scored more goals than the other could score, even if it were to complete its five kicks, no more kicks are taken*
- *If after both teams have taken five kicks, both have scored the same number of goals, or have not scored any goals, kicks continue to be taken in the same order until one team has scored a goal more than the other from*

the same number of kicks
- *A goalkeeper who is injured while kicks are being taken from the penalty mark and is unable to continue as goalkeeper may be replaced by a named substitute provided his team has not used the maximum number of substitutes permitted under the competition rules*
- *With the exception of the foregoing case, only players who are on the field of play at the end of the match, which includes extra time where appropriate, are allowed to take kicks from the penalty mark*
- *Each kick is taken by a different player and all eligible players must take a kick before any player can take a second kick*
- *An eligible player may change places with the goalkeeper at any time when kicks from the penalty mark are being taken*
- *Only the eligible players and match officials are permitted to remain on the field of play when kicks from the penalty mark are being taken*
- *All players, except the player*

taking the kick and the two goalkeepers must remain within the centre circle

● *The goalkeeper who is the kicker's team-mate must remain on the field of play, outside the penalty area in which the kicks are being taken, behind the penalty area border line which*

runs parallel with the goal line and at least 9.15 m (10 yds) from the penalty mark

● *Unless otherwise stated, the relevant Laws of the Game and International F.A. Board Decisions apply when kicks from the penalty mark are being taken.*

Fair Play in Sport

Definition

Fair Play is a code of conduct which respects both the written and the unwritten rules of the game and treats opponents as partners in sport.

Fair Play is expressed through spontaneous actions which applaud sporting excellence, show concern for opponents in distress, acknowledge defeat with dignity and victory with humility.

Sport with fair play enriches the quality of life.

The Fair Play Trophy, created by the French sculptor Jean Ipoustéguy, is inscribed 'mieux qu'une victoire' - 'better than a victory'.

Chivalrous help at the final match.
Italy - Germany FR in Madrid before the very eyes of the Brazilian referee.

Glossary

Advantage:	An offence has been committed but the referee allows play to continue so that the offending team does not gain an advantage.
Assistant Referee	A match official, with a patrol outside a touch line, who signals with a flag when the ball has crossed a boundary line and undertakes any other duties delegated by the referee.
Attacker:	Any player in the opponents' half of the field.
Caution:	An official warning against continued misconduct or foul play. Indicated by the referee displaying a yellow card.
Centre circle:	A circle of 10 yards (9.15 metres) radius drawn from a mark in the centre of the field.
Centre mark:	A mark in the centre of the field from which a kick off is taken.
Charging:	Shoulder-to-shoulder contact to put an opponent off balance in order to obtain or retain possession of the ball.
Coach:	A team official who may convey tactical instructions to players during a match.
Corner area:	The area contained within the corner arc of 1 yard (1 metre) radius drawn from each corner of the field.

Corner kick:	A direct free kick taken from the corner area after the ball has crossed the goal line, outside of the goal, having been last touched by a player of the defending team.
Curtain Raiser:	A minor match played immediately before a major match, usually an international.
Dangerous Play:	Any act considered by the referee to be dangerous to an opponent.
Defender:	Any player in his own half of the field.
Direct Free Kick:	A free-kick from which a goal may be scored if the ball goes directly into the goal unless taken by the defending team.
Drop Ball:	The ball is dropped by the referee to restart play after it has been stopped for a reason other than an offence by a player.
Extra Time:	An additional period of play to obtain a result after a match is drawn. Usually 30 minutes divided into two halves.
Fourth Official:	A substitute referee or assistant referee.
Free Kick:	Awarded for an offence by the opposing team. A kick at the ball free from obstruction by opponents. May be Direct or Indirect - see separate entries.
Goal:	The targets, comprising two upright posts and a joining cross-bar, placed at each end of the field through which the ball must pass to score a goal.
Goal Area:	An area, 6 x 20 yards (5.5 x 18.3 metres), marked in front of each goal.
Goalkeeper:	The only player in each team to have the privilege of handling the ball inside his own penalty area. Dressed in colours to distinguish him from other players.

Goal Kick: Method of restarting play after the ball has crossed the goal line, outside of the goal, having been last touched by a player of the attacking team.

Goal Line: The boundary line at each end of the field on which the goals are placed.

Halfway line: A line drawn across the centre of the field.

Hand Ball: An offence when a hand or any part of an arm, up to the shoulder joint, is used with the intention of touching the ball.

Holding: Intentional use of the arms to physically obstruct an opponent.

Indirect Free Kick: A free kick from which a goal cannot be scored direct. The ball must touch a player, other than the kicker, before a goal can be scored.

International FA Board: The governing body for the Laws of the Game.

Jumping at an Opponent: An offence when a player jumps at an opponent intentionally to prevent him from playing the ball.

Kick Off: A kick off, taken from the centre of the field to start the game, to restart after half-time and after each goal is scored.

Misconduct: Any act of misbehaviour contrary to the letter and spirit of the Laws of the Game.

National Association: The recognised governing body for soccer in the country concerned.

Obstruction/Impeding: An offence when a player, who is not playing the ball, intentionally runs between an opponent and the ball or interposes his body to impede progress.

Offside: An offence when a player, in an offside position, is considered by the referee to be interfering with play or an opponent.

Offside Position: A player is in an offside position if he is nearer to his opponents' goal-line than the ball unless: (a) he is in his own half, or (b) he has at least two opponents either level with him or nearer to the goal line.

Outside Agency: Any agency which is not part of the game.

Penalty Arc: An arc drawn outside the penalty area with a radius of 10 yards (9.15 metres) from the penalty mark. It indicates the minimum distance from the ball which must be observed by all players at a penalty kick excepting the kicker and goalkeeper.

Penalty Area: An area, 18 x 44 yards (16.5 x 40.3 metres), marked in front of each goal.

Penalty Mark: The place from which penalty kicks are taken 12 yards (11 metres) from the midpoint of the goal line.

Referee: An official appointed to supervise and control a game usually with two assistants.

Result: The team scoring the greater number of goals is the winner; if no goals or an equal number of goals are scored, the game is a "draw".

Serious Foul-play: Usually applies to any of the direct free kick offences, listed in Law 12, being committed in a serious manner.

Substitute: A non-participating player who may be called upon to replace a participating player.

Throw-in: The method of restarting play when the ball has passed out of bounds over a touch line.

Tie-breaker: A system used to determine the winning team when a match is drawn in a knock-out competition. It comprises a series of kicks from the penalty-mark.

Touch Line: The boundary line at each side of the field.

Tripping an Opponent: Bringing down, or attempting to bring down, an opponent by the use of the legs or by stooping in front of or behind him.

Violent Conduct: Any violent act of a physical or moral nature.

Questions and Answers to The Laws of the Game

A selection of official questions from National Associations together with answers approved by The International Football Association Board.

Law 1 - The Field of Play

Q.   For a corner kick, is it permitted to mark the nearest distance which must be kept by players of the opposing team?

A.   Yes, if it is marked outside the field of play, at right angles and at a specific distance from the goal line and touch line respectively and at 9.15 metres (10 yards) from the edge of the corner arc.

Q.   If a goalkeeper draws unauthorised marks on the field of play with his foot, what action should the referee take?

A.   If the referee notices that this is being done during the match, he need not interrupt the game just to caution the player who is making unauthorised marks on the field of play after the match has started. The player concerned must be cautioned for unsporting behaviour when there is an interruption in the game. If, however, the referee notices this before the match starts, then he shall caution the offending player immediately.

Law 3 - The Number of Players

Q.   If a player in possession of the ball passes over the touch line, or the goal line, without the ball in order to beat an opponent, should the referee penalise him for leaving the field of play without permission?

A.   No. Going outside the field of play may be considered as part of a playing movement, but players are expected, as a general rule, to remain within the playing area.

Q.   May an expelled player stay on the substitutes bench?

A.   No. An expelled player shall return to the dressing room.

Q.   Is a substitute considered to be a member of the team at the moment he enters the field of play or when the referee restarts the game?

A.   The substitution is completed when the substitute enters the field of play, provided the game has been stopped, the player being replaced has left the field and the referee has signalled his permission for the substitute to enter the field of play at the halfway line.

Law 4 - The Players' Equipment

Q.   If a player, following doctor's orders, protects his elbow or any similar part of his body with a bandage to prevent further injury, has the referee the power to decide if the bandage constitutes a danger to other players?

A.   Yes.

Q.   If the colour of the shirts of the two goalkeepers is the same, what should the referee do if neither has another shirt to change into?

A.   The referee shall allow play to continue.

Law 5 - The Referee

Q.   Is the referee empowered to order team officials away from the boundary lines of the field of play?

A.   Yes, the referee has the right to take such measures even if the match is being played on a public ground.

Q.   Does a team captain have the right to question a decision of the referee?

A.   No, neither the captain nor any other player has the right to show disagreement with a decision taken by the referee.

Law 7 - The Duration of the Match

Q.   Is it left to the referee's discretion to decide whether lost time (injuries or other causes) are to be compensated or not?

A. No, the referee must add on in each half of the game all time lost. However, the amount of such time is at the discretion of the referee.

Law 8 - The Start and Restart of Play

Q. If the ball is kicked straight into the opponents' goal from the kickoff, what decision does the referee give?

A. A goal.

Law 9 - The Ball in and out of Play

Q. Is the ball out of play if any part of the ball overlaps either the goal line or the touch line?

A. No, the whole of the ball must cross the line.

Q. The ball accidentally hits the referee or a linesman on the field of play and rebounds into goal. What should the referee's decision be?

A. The referee shall award the goal.

Law 10 - The Method of Scoring

Q. If a referee signals a goal before the ball has passed wholly over the goal line and he immediately realises his error, is the goal valid?

A. No. The game shall be restarted by dropping the ball on that part of the goal area line, parallel to the goal line, nearest to the place where it was when the referee inadvertently stopped play.

Law 11 - Off-side

Q. Does a player infringe the law if he is in an off-side position and moves a little way beyond the boundary of the field of play to show clearly to the referee that he is not interfering with play?

A. No, but if the referee considers that such a move has a tactical aim or is in any way a feint, and the player takes part in the game immediately after, the referee may deem his action to be unsporting behaviour and caution him. Play shall be restarted in accordance with the Laws of the Game.

Q. What action should the referee take if a defending player moves beyond his own goal line in order to place an opponent in an offside position?

A.   The action of the defender is considered as unsporting behaviour, but it is not necessary for the referee to stop play immediately to caution the player. The attacker should not be punished for the position in which he has been unfairly placed.

Law 12 - Fouls and Misconduct

Q.   What action should the referee take if a player of the defending team, other than the goalkeeper, standing outside the penalty area, intentionally handles the ball within the penalty area?

A.   He shall penalise the player by awarding the penalty kick because the offence took place within the penalty area.

Q.   If a referee cautions a player who in turn apologises for his misconduct, can the referee omit to report the incident?

A.   No, all cautions must be reported.

Q.   What action should the referee take against players who leave the field while celebrating a goal?

A.   Celebrating a goal is all part of football. A caution is only warranted if a player gives an excessive demonstration of jubilation, e.g. by jumping over the boundary fence, gesticulating at his opponents or the spectators or ridiculing them by pointing to his shirt.

Q.   How should a player be penalised for throwing an object (stone, shoe) or spitting from within the penalty-area at a player who is outside the penalty area?

A.   He must be penalised by a penalty kick and be sent off.

Q.   Is there a difference in the punishment to be given for spitting at an opponent or attempting to do so?

A.   No. Spitting or attempting to do so are equally grave offences.

Law 13 - Free-kicks

Q.   When taking a free kick awarded to their team, may players use feinting tactics to confuse opponents?

A.   Yes. Furthermore, if the opponents move nearer than 9.15 metres (10 yards) to the ball before it is in play, they shall be cautioned.

Q.   A player wishes to play a free kick quickly with an opponent being only 4.5 metres from the ball. Should the referee allow this?

A. Yes, and even if an opponent intercepts the ball, play shall be allowed to continue.

Law 14 - The Penalty-kick

Q. If a player takes a penalty kick before the referee has signalled, what action should the referee take?

A. The kick must be retaken. The player shall be cautioned only if he takes the penalty kick again without awaiting the referee's signal.

Q. Does taking kicks from the penalty mark to determine the winner of a match form part of the match?

A. Such kicks from the penalty mark never form part of a match.

Law 15 - Throw-in

Q. Is there a maximum distance away from the touch line from which a throw-in may be taken?

A. No. A throw-in should be taken from the place where the ball left the field of play. However, a distance of up to one metre from the exact position is a common practical guideline.

Q. If an opponent stands in front of a player at a throw-in to impede him, what action should the referee take?

A. Allow the throw-in to be taken if the opponent remains stationary. But if he moves or gesticulates to distract the thrower, he shall be cautioned for unsporting behaviour.

Law 16 - The Goal-kick

Q. If a player is intentionally tripped before the ball passes outside of the penalty area when a goal kick is being taken, should a free kick be awarded?

A. No, the ball is not in play until it has been out of the penalty area. The offender shall be cautioned or sent off and the goal kick retaken.

A booklet containing over 150 official Questions and Answers, including the foregoing, is available from FIFA.